SIMPLY CLEAN

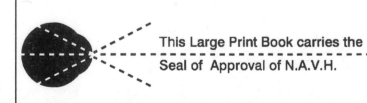

This Large Print Book carries the
Seal of Approval of N.A.V.H.

To my husband and kiddos —
there's no one else
I'd rather do this life with,
messes and all

CONTENTS

Part Two:
The 7-Day Simply Clean Kick Start: 10 Minutes to a Happier, Healthier Home

Part Three:
The 28-Day Simply Clean Challenge: Turn the Method into a Habit

Part Four:
Customizing the Simply Clean
Method for Your Life

Part Five:
How to Clean and Organize
(Just About) Anything

16

Part Six:
Cleaning Supplies and Resources

INTRODUCTION

What if I told you that you could spend just 10 minutes a day on cleaning and organizing and you'd have a serene home all week long? That those mundane tasks like laundry and loading the dishwasher could become effortless? That you could become one of those people who welcomes unexpected visitors, because you know your space always looks tidy?

Well, it's true. I can show you how to turn cleaning into an easy, stress-free activity that can be done in just 10 minutes a day. In fact, I can even show you how to enjoy cleaning. Because yes, cleaning can be relaxing, and it can be fun!

If you're feeling overwhelmed and don't know where to start, forget everything you thought you knew about keeping a clean house. It's perfectly normal to loathe or resent cleaning. You've let it control your life, and you've set it on a reactive mode instead of an automatic mode. Let's change that!

Homekeeping is a learned behavior. During the past eight years I have coached millions of readers through my online community, Clean Mama. The questions and emails I receive on a daily basis are proof positive that an overwhelming number of people don't know how to keep a home clean and maintained. And I get that! No one is born knowing how to get water rings off of furniture or the easiest way to clean a slipcover. In these pages, I will show you where to start and how to *keep* a clean home — simply and easily.

I first established this routine when I was an art teacher. I picked up quite a few odd jobs, one of which was cleaning my fellow teachers' houses after school. I found an odd satisfaction in cleaning other people's homes, and it was fun to experiment with different techniques and try the products they used. I assumed that it would be just this easy and fun to keep my own home clean when I had one. Little did I know, cleaning your own home isn't nearly as easy (or fun) as cleaning someone else's. When cleaning someone else's house, you have laser focus and you get in, do the job, and get out. When cleaning your own home there are distractions and traps to fall into. For instance, you decide to clean the kitchen. You're just getting started and the phone rings. The phone call derails your kitchen cleaning and you've lost track of time and now it's time for dinner. There's a pile of things to go through and you put it off until another day. Focus is essential to cleaning — I didn't realize this right away but you'll see how this mindset makes sense moving forward.

When my husband and I were first married, we had the most darling little apartment. It was a one bedroom, small, and just right. Despite its size, I still found it difficult to keep up with everything that had to be done while being gone every day at work. It was during this time when I was sick of cleaning and doing laundry over the weekend that I started to develop a simplified approach to cleaning.

I did my own market research, asking family and friends how they structured chores and housekeeping while reading up on how different people approached keeping a clean house. It seemed like most people cleaned all weekend and resented it. Some talked about things like washing day and market day and house cleaning day. This resonated with me. I liked the nostalgic approach, but the tasks didn't really work for me. I tried cleaning the apartment all at once and tidying during the week. This was great when it was clean but if we were extra busy or someone got sick, the place fell apart quickly. Next I tried assigning specific tasks to days and setting a timer to see if I could clean more quickly or just as well working a little differently. This was better, but I still had laundry piling up because I was doing laundry once during the week. It was just my husband and me, but I didn't always get it all put away. (I've always been a laundry procrastinator.) Determined to figure this cleaning routine thing out, I kept switching things around and trying different approaches until I finally got into a groove and our darling apartment sparkled most of the time. I was relieved and so excited that I could keep our home clean all week long. Laundry, a spotless kitchen, clean floors, and a clean bathroom were pretty much all I had to concentrate on, but it worked and I felt like I had conquered the homekeeping world. Ha!

Time to take the approach to the next level. A town house. Two levels, two bedrooms, and still working two to three jobs. The routine was still working, but being thrown into a new place with projects turned my routine on its side. Once everything was painted and put away, it was time to figure out how to keep the town house just as neat and tidy as the little apartment.

The space seemed to get dirty by itself and needed quite a bit more upkeep than that little apartment. Daily tasks became my focus. What was I doing every day or what should I be doing every day? I determined that making the bed, cleaning the kitchen, and making sure the clothes were in the hamper were top priorities. Once I had these things mastered I started adding little things and soon the town house was cleaning itself, so to speak.

Fast forward a bit to a new baby and working full-time. Things got interesting, but I tweaked and perfected my routine to be more manageable and take even less time. I didn't want to spend the little time we had at home with our daughter cleaning. Later I was able to leave teaching and stay at home with our two babies, but the cleaning routine wasn't super easy to maintain. I was exhausted; the main goal at this stage was to keep things that could be ingested by little ones off the floor and to make sure everyone had at least one clean outfit to wear. I would go back and forth between just daily tasks and adding another job when I had time. Guess what emerged from the exhaustion? A cleaning routine that worked for me! I chose one specific task each day, in addition to my daily cleaning tasks. I figured if I could get to that one task, it would feel like I had done something. And something felt better than nothing. Surprisingly, this simple plan actually kept the house clean. I couldn't believe it. Armed with a plan, I no longer had to worry about what looked the worst or what a visitor would see first, I just did my daily and weekly tasks in a couple minutes (still setting that timer) and enjoyed the babies the rest of the day.

If I've learned anything, it's that a schedule will never be perfect forever, but this routine worked for me in so many circumstances — working outside the home without kids, stay-at-home mom with one and then two babies under two. I started blogging and building a business and working from home — it still worked. Then the true test? I went back to work more than full-time and traveled for my job and had my business on the side. It was an incredibly busy and hectic time in our lives, but there was the stability of knowing what to clean and when to clean it. I knew that on Saturdays there would be clean sheets on the beds and the bathrooms would be clean on Monday. I love that little bit of structure in the midst of everyday life. The true test of the routine? When I was pregnant with my third and working both jobs. Amazingly, it still worked. Granted, the house wasn't as tidy as it had been in the past, but it only took a little bit of time and effort to whip it into shape.

I've put the work in and field-tested these methods in just about every scenario. I only work for myself now, but with three active kids it's imperative that the housework takes only minutes every day.

As a cleaning expert, I have tested and tried just about every cleaning product, remedy, and method under the sun, and I love sharing what I've found. Better yet, I love hearing that the rings on the furniture disappeared and the stains on the slipcover are gone!

Over the years, I've developed a routine — now used by thousands of people — to clean just a little every day so that your home is always spic-and-span.

So, if you feel overwhelmed about keeping a clean house while still enjoying your family and life, you've come to the right place! The Simply Clean method is meant for busy lives, and it's designed to take the drudgery right out of cleaning. Sometimes we want someone to tell us what to do. Set it and forget it. Tell me what to clean, when to clean it, and how to clean it. That's the way I feel, too, which is why I came up with the routine in the first place. It isn't complicated, and there's plenty of room for life's mishaps, with a day to catch up every week.

If you can spend 10 minutes every day on a few daily tasks and 1 hour each week on weekly tasks (like laundry), your home will be cleaner than it was the day before and realistically, that's what matters, right? With this system running on autopilot in your home, you can save your energy and time for the fun stuff: hanging out with your family, keeping up with a hobby, reading a favorite book, or catching up on a TV show.

In the following chapters, you'll also find:

 QUICK TIPS: Simple tips that make life easier. You'll find them interspersed throughout the book right alongside other instructions on the same topic.

We'll start by setting some realistic goals for homekeeping and carve out a couple of minutes every day that can be used to do a little cleaning. Take it one step, day, or task at a time and fight through any "overwhelm." The overwhelm is what stops you in your tracks and keeps you from moving forward. Or maybe it's the spilled gallon of milk on the floor? Whatever has stopped you before doesn't stand a chance now, because this time you have a simple plan, ready for any curveballs that life throws.

You'll put together a simple cleaning caddy or two for your home, and then we'll get started with the 7-Day Simply Clean Kick Start, designed to motivate anyone to jump into a cleaning routine. After this kick start, you will have cleared the clutter, collected the tools you need, and already put a few simple techniques into practice. Once you've completed the kick start you may be tempted to relax and enjoy your hard work, but I will encourage you to continue with the simple daily tasks until they have become routine. You can repeat the kick start if you need another week to get in the groove, but I'm guessing you'll be excited to move on to the next step: the 28-Day Simply Clean Challenge.

The challenge is designed to help you build the habits needed to make cleaning effortless, so you never have to really think about it again. I'll show you exactly how to layer the monthly tasks into your newly established weekly routine. Make it a game or a goal and challenge yourself to follow the checklists, rely on the resources, and see how much you can accomplish with just a few minutes of focused cleaning a day. You'll be surprised by how much you can enjoy the soothing, methodical side of cleaning once you're not stressed and overwhelmed by it!

After you've completed the 7-Day Kick Start and the 28-Day Simply Clean Challenge, you're ready to continue following the Simply Clean method, or you can customize it to your particular circumstances. Whether you live alone or with a family of twelve, you work outside the home or not, live in a big-city studio apartment or a country home, I can show you exactly how to make the routine work for you.

And because I couldn't leave you without some pretty and fresh-smelling cleaning supplies, I've also included a little mini guide with recipes for making your own cleaners using simple pantry items you may already have on hand. With these organic, eco-friendly cleaning recipes, you'll save money on expensive products, reduce the chemical residue in your home, and do a good thing for the planet. Did I mention that they smell wonderful and look pretty in a nice spray bottle? My guess is that you'll want to skip to this section first to mix up a little lemon-clove sink scrub or lavender all-purpose cleaning spray!

Ready to find a way to accomplish the

mundane tasks of homekeeping and actually enjoy it? Armed with this book, a cute caddy, and a step-by-step plan, you'll be on your way to a simply clean and inviting home that you can enjoy every single day!

■ ■ ■ ■

PART ONE: THE SIMPLY CLEAN METHOD: THE SECRET TO CLEANING LESS, YET HAVING A CLEANER HOME

■ ■ ■ ■

CHAPTER ONE:
YOU WANT A CLEAN AND TIDY HOME. NOW WHAT?

If you've longed for a cleaning routine and a little more structure in your homekeeping, you're not alone. Most of us crave some type of structure and sometimes it's just nice to know that bathrooms will get cleaned each week. Or maybe you've tried a handful of cleaning routines and none of them worked when life happened and someone got sick, or you were at work all day and just didn't feel like cleaning, or you were going to clean the fridge when you got home from work but another mess took priority. Maybe you fell off the cleaning bandwagon, felt defeated, and ended up going back to cleaning on Saturdays or just when you couldn't stand the mess anymore.

So are you doomed to avoid cleaning routines forever? I can most definitely give you a resounding NO. Sometimes a fresh start and a renewed perspective can lead to a different mindset. Don't be afraid to try this approach. It's a new way of cleaning and caring for your home. Give it some time and you'll quickly find that it's more about the plan than the work itself. Stick with me, follow along, and the little bit of work you put in will be worth it. I pinky-swear promise. Okay, maybe that's a little lame, but trust me, the Simply Clean method works and you'll be so glad you gave it a whirl!

WHY OTHER CLEANING METHODS DON'T WORK, BUT SIMPLY CLEAN DOES

Here's what I think about cleaning, routines, clutter, and mess: they're part of life. You create the mess (or someone you love does) and it needs to be cleaned up. Cause and effect. The difference with the Simply Clean method is that it requires only a few simple actions that make sense every day. After a few weeks, maybe with a reminder on your phone or calendar, it's committed to memory and that action starts to become a habit. That habit quietly turns into something that you "just do" and then, once you're doing it, it *is* simply clean. The bedroom, the kitchen, the bathroom — they practically clean themselves. So how do you get there?

WHERE TO START, PLUS HOW TO AVOID "OVERWHELM"

It's important to just start somewhere. Starting the process and doing something, anything, is more helpful than doing everything. Doing everything merely leads to burnout and cleaning fatigue. Think of it like deciding to eliminate coffee from your diet in one fell swoop: The first day you do it, you endure the headache and wake up the second day ready to continue this new habit. You almost make it all the way through day two, until the splitting headache wins and you give in to the caffeine and the coffee drive-thru lures you in and you decide that you're just going to keep drinking coffee and forget about curbing your caffeine addiction. In retrospect, quitting coffee might have been easier if you broke down the process into more manageable steps. Instead of quitting cold turkey, going from two cups a day down to one cup a day may have been an easier transition. Starting a new cleaning routine is very similar: you start strong but get busy, someone gets sick, or you just plain don't feel like folding another load of laundry and that one tiny load piles up to a mountain of four. Let's keep this easy, seamless, and doable — a cleaning routine that runs itself with just a couple steps every day. And the best part? If you miss a day or a task, you can make it up *or not* — it's up to you.

The most effective part of the Simply Clean method is that *you will not feel overwhelmed by the routine.* You'll feel like it's helping you get your home to a manageable place where just about any real-life circumstance can be thrown at you and you can still get the bathrooms clean. Every day of the week has a task, and if you don't get to that task, guess what? You *skip* it and move on to the next day. No guilt, no making it up, just move on.

For a perfectionist, this is a really difficult concept to embrace. Most weeks I don't get to everything on my list. This can feel defeating unless you have a plan and expect that not everything will get done. Accept it, set goals, and don't worry about the completion of that list. Simply do your best and do what you can — it's that easy. How can you just move on without cleaning the bathrooms or dusting or vacuuming? Because every single Friday is a day to catch up on any uncompleted tasks. If you don't get to the task on Friday because the week was crazy or Friday you were working out of town or something else came up, you table the task until its day appears on the calendar the following week. This is the magic of the Simply Clean method and why I believe it really works for so many households with different schedules and circumstances.

EMBRACE A LITTLE MESS NOW AND THEN

Your home will most likely never be show-ready all the time. Life is messy. Just when I feel like I've reached the brink of what I can handle with Legos and blocks strewn from one end of the house to the other, I take a deep breath and remember that these annoying toys will soon be replaced with other things like sports and activity equipment and then car keys and cell phones. My little ones won't be little for very long; and while some days the mess gets the best of me, I know it's a good thing.

I have "clutter" written on my daily to-do list. Every. Single. Day. Papers, magazines, books, toys, clothes — those things that pile up and make me (maybe you, too?) feel a little bit crazy. You'll learn how to deal with those quickly and efficiently every day. Those little messes will never pile up to become big, unmanageable messes because you are dealing with them daily, and that daily contact is all that's needed to curb and contain the stress and anxiety that come with trying to manage a home. The Simply Clean method will give you the space to embrace your messy life and not be overwhelmed by it.

PRIORITIZING AND HONEST GOAL SETTING (BECAUSE IT'S OKAY TO NOT DO IT ALL!)

What made you decide to read this book in the first place? What do you need in your life to feel like your home isn't swirling in chaos? What are some things that have been annoying you when you walk in the door every evening? You know you have to do them but you've been putting them off for far too long. Maybe you want to stop doing all the laundry over the weekends or you want to clear out that junk drawer. Take a minute to be honest with yourself and write down three goals you'd like to accomplish in the next couple months. Clean and organize the whole house are not the kind of goals I want you to set. Make the goals things that are quick, simple, attainable. You're going to be making huge strides over the course of this book, but consistency is going to be the key to overcoming any prior misconceptions about how difficult it is to keep a clean house. It's easy and your goals should be, too. Make the bed almost every day or stay on top of the laundry. Simple, action-able goals that can be completed with a little time and effort are all you need to write down.

1. _____
2. _____
3. _____

If you're feeling overwhelmed and don't know where to start, forget everything you thought you knew about keeping a clean house.

The secret to cleaning less and having a cleaner home is simple: have a plan. You might be thinking, *I bought this book for someone to tell me that I need a plan?* Or maybe you're thinking, *I've tried that and it lasted for three days.* Don't worry, the secret to a cleaner home in less time is more than just a plan, it's the Simply Clean method. Not only does it work, it will most likely revolutionize how you see your home and your cleaning routine.

CLEANING ROUTINES: WHY YOU NEED ONE

A cleaning routine may sound complicated and rigid, and many are, but the Simply Clean method actually works because it's flexible and workable with just about every schedule.

What's different about the Simply Clean method? There's grace built right in to the routine to ensure success. Even if you think that you can't be helped by a cleaning routine or that you don't need one, think back to a particularly stressful time in your life. What was the first thing that you stopped doing? I'm going to go out on a limb and say cleaning. I'll be the first one to tell you that that's normal and expected. But I also want to tell you that when you let go of things like washing dishes and you let the laundry pile up, those piles might have contributed to your stress. I'm here to encourage you to let go of some things when things get crazy, but not everything. Have your own personal musts list and do those or half of those, or even one of those. A little order goes a long way to keeping the sanity.

 QUICK TIP: Feeling overwhelmed or stressed over the state of a room or your whole house? Choose one surface and completely clear it, clean it, and put what was on that surface where it belongs. Relax, take a deep breath, and move on.

Just Start Somewhere:
Every Day a Little Something

My cleaning mantra is "Every day a little something." It's a great reminder to do something every single day. Embrace that mindset, and you'll be halfway to making a cleaning routine work for you and your schedule. Have you ever looked around your home, looked at a room in complete disarray, a cluttered counter, a mountain of laundry, or an unfinished project and felt so defeated that you were practically paralyzed? That defeated feeling is what keeps you from managing your cleaning tasks like a professional. Instead of looking around at all that you have to do, simply choose something from the daily tasks and get to work. Set a timer and work for 5 minutes in the morning and 5 minutes in the evening or just 10 minutes all at once. Or if you're home during the day, split that time up in 5-minute increments around mealtimes to keep it really easy. Those simple daily tasks? Chances are you're already doing them. Let's put them into motion and give them a little automation for success in your home.

Daily Cleaning Tasks in
Just 10–15 Minutes a Day

Chances are you know that folding and putting that laundry away would be a good idea and dealing with that stack of mail instead of letting it pile up is probably the right choice, right? But do you know why you aren't putting those tasks into motion? I'm guessing it's because you haven't really thought about it or you're just too busy to care. Does that sound harsh? I hope not, I hope it sounds realistic and honest. I created this cleaning routine because I figured there *has* to be a way to keep a house clean most of the time with minimal effort. Trust me here and get ready to jump in to the simplest and most effective cleaning routine you can imagine.

Let's get started with the daily tasks — they're the secret to keeping your home clean most of the time. The five daily tasks are things that you might be doing already but if you feel overwhelmed by them, start gradually and add one a week until you've added all five in.

1. **Make beds.** Quickly pull up your bedding and fluff those pillows as soon as you can in the morning. This will help set your mind for the day — your bed is made, hooray! If you have children, teach them at an early age how to make their own beds. Don't go back and correct their work, just let it be. I've found

that using just a bottom sheet and a washable duvet cover or quilt is the easiest way to make a bed. Just quickly pull the duvet or quilt up, toss the pillows on top, and it's an instantly made bed!

QUICK TIP: If it's hard to wrap your mind around not using a top sheet, I get it! But I've found that washable duvet covers are a major time-saver in our house. Making the bed is easier for everyone, especially children, and it saves time when changing sheets.

2. **Check floors.** This is simple — just sweep or vacuum as needed. In my house, it seems like the broom comes out after every meal, but it's a quick sweep under the kitchen table and it's put away. If the day is a busy one, I might look past the floor until after dinner and just drag out the broom once. If you have pets, you might need to grab that vacuum cleaner or broom a little more often, especially if it's shedding season. Any sweeping or vacuuming that's done on a daily basis is

merely for touch-up purposes; no thorough vacuuming is necessary.

 QUICK TIP: If you have little ones, get a small broom and dustpan and let them clean up their own food messes. Not only are you teaching them to clean but you are also giving them a responsibility. Keep the broom accessible and you'll probably find them reaching for it all by themselves.

3. **Wipe counters.** Wipe down your kitchen counters after meals if needed, and at least once a day, after dinner. Check the bathroom counters to make sure that they are clean and cleared off daily. If you're in the habit of keeping makeup and beauty supplies out on your counters, consider putting them in a basket or drawer to keep the counters clear and easy to clean. A quick walk through the bathroom(s) in your home with a cleaning wipe or microfiber cloth and your favorite cleaner is all you need to do. Look for those little messes like toothpaste in the sink and any grunge on the counters. Keeping

the counters wiped down daily makes it easier to maintain a clean home, and who doesn't love clear counters?

QUICK TIP: If you aren't home during the day, simply wipe down counters as needed before leaving the house and/or at the end of the day if necessary.

4. **Declutter.** Pick up clutter during the day as you see it. This also includes dealing with mail on a daily basis as well as keeping counters and floors picked up. It doesn't take much for clutter to creep in and invade your home. I find that dealing with it daily is the only way to avoid the overwhelming feeling that comes from a pile of papers on the kitchen counter or a pile of shoes at the door. Teach other family members how to deal with clutter by putting systems in place to manage the incoming papers, keys, shoes, clothes and anything else that adds to your clutter quotient. Simple items like a basket where the clothes pile up, a dish where keys get set, and a tray for incoming and outgoing mail and papers

will go a long way to keep the inevitable clutter in its proper place. Having these systems in place will turn visual noise into visual serenity.

5. **Do laundry.** Do one load of laundry from start to folded and put away *every single day.* I think you'll be surprised at how manageable it is. Simplify your laundry routine by using just the basics. No need for an arsenal of laundry supplies — pare it down to a couple favorites and keep those stocked. My best tip for laundry? Delegate! Teach your family members how to do laundry and you'll be cutting your laundry time in half in no time. If you don't have a washer and dryer and use a Laundromat or communal laundry room, this is most likely not feasible. But you can easily do a larger amount of laundry by running multiple machines at the same time. Use this to your advantage and plan it out. Keep a divided hamper or multiple baskets for your laundry storage so you can quickly toss your linens in the machines and get your loads running. Fold your laundry right away and put it away as soon as you return to home to avoid the laundry basket stare down.

DAILY CLEANING TASKS CHECKLIST			
	✓		✓
Make beds		Make beds	
Check floors		Check floors	
Wipe counters		Wipe counters	
Declutter		Declutter	
Do laundry		Do laundry	
Make beds		Make beds	
Check floors		Check floors	
Wipe counters		Wipe counters	
Declutter		Declutter	
Do laundry		Do laundry	
Make beds		Make beds	
Check floors		Check floors	
Wipe counters		Wipe counters	
Declutter		Declutter	
Do laundry		Do laundry	
Make beds		Make beds	
Check floors		Check floors	
Wipe counters		Wipe counters	
Declutter		Declutter	
Do laundry		Do laundry	
Make beds		Make beds	
Check floors		Check floors	
Wipe counters		Wipe counters	
Declutter		Declutter	
Do laundry		Do laundry	

QUICK TIP: Stop buying multiple types of socks! Choose a favorite white sock for most days and have at least seven pairs of that sock. No need to fold; if you'd like to skip that step, simply put them all in a basket or small container that fits in a dresser drawer.

WEEKLY TASKS

Daily cleaning tasks go hand in hand with weekly cleaning tasks. Completed separately they will both help keep your home cleaner, but when completed together regularly, you'll see the most progress. Please don't think that you have to accomplish everything on the list — simply set your timer for 10–15 minutes a day and do what you can. Everyone's busy and no one really wants to spend more time than necessary cleaning toilets or doing laundry. Finding a simple way to complete and implement household tasks is key.

Monday — Bathroom Cleaning Day

Every Monday I clean bathrooms. I don't wash the bathroom floors because I wash them on Thursdays — I find that this really cuts down on bathroom cleaning time. I like to keep my bathroom cleaning supplies in each bathroom; you might prefer to tote a cleaning bucket or caddy from bathroom to bathroom. See Chapter 2 for tips on assembling a well-stocked bathroom caddy.

 QUICK TIP: Get the worst job out of the way on Mondays by getting the bathrooms fresh and clean for the week ahead.

Tuesday — Dusting Day

Looking for the best way to dust? Work from the top down and quickly go through the house dusting all the hard surfaces, staircases and railings, TVs and furniture. When you are doing weekly dusting, move quickly. If you have extra time, add a deep-clean dusting with polish or fit in rotating cleaning tasks like dusting light fixtures or ceiling fans.

Rule 1 for me is to only keep out things that we love and need. If it just collects dust, it's not worth moving every week to dust under it. With little kids around, I have a minimal amount of stuff on display just so I don't have to worry about anything happening to it. Uncluttered surfaces make dusting so much easier. If you look around and think, I thought I just dusted this? Dust weekly and you'll spend less time dusting and you won't be playing the white glove game.

I prefer to use microfiber cloths and a dusting mitt. I also use an extendable-reach duster for cobwebs and hard-to-reach ceilings and corners. This can be an expensive tool, but if you have lots of tall ceilings it's worth it. I also use a natural beeswax cream to polish and condition some furniture monthly or as needed. See Chapter 2 for tips on assembling a well-stocked dusting caddy.

 QUICK TIP: If you like the spray-and-wipe dusting method for furniture, spray directly on a microfiber cloth and dust to a shine. This will avoid overspray on floors and it will keep you from using more spray than you need to. Look for a nontoxic furniture spray so you avoid that waxy buildup that eventually ruins furniture.

Wednesday — Vacuuming Day

On Wednesdays I haul out the Hoover and vacuum all the carpets in the house. Curious why it makes sense to vacuum on Wednesdays? Tuesday is dusting day so Wednesday is the day to clean up the dust from Tuesday. Simple as that. Move quickly — start on the second floor with the room that's the farthest away from the stairs. If you have a one-level home, start at the corner farthest from the front door. Vacuum bedrooms, bathrooms, hallways, and stairs. The main goal of vacuuming is to get the dust and dirt out of your home by doing a thorough job once a week. Vacuum in between as needed, but a weekly session ensures that all the dust and pet hair is picked up and the floors are ready for washing on Thursday.

QUICK TIP: If and when you need a new vacuum cleaner, make sure you get one with attachments— they'll make your cleaning life so much easier. Look for a crevice tool, an upholstery attachment, and a soft bristle brush that you can use on blinds and windows.

I wash floors on Thursdays because all the hard floors were vacuumed or swept on Wednesday. Yes, it would be more optimal to vacuum and wash floors all on the same day, but I just don't have that kind of time and I'm guessing you probably don't either. So let's just split it up and vacuum on Wednesdays and wash floors on Thursdays. Alternatively, you can do one floor or section of the house on Wednesday and the other on Thursday. The point is to make sure that your floors are clean by the end of the day on Thursdays.

There are so many floor cleaning products and tools on the market — find one that fits your budget and that you will enjoy using. I recommend using floor tools that have removable microfiber mop heads or pads. If you like making your own cleaners or want to choose what goes in your floor cleaner, choose one with a refillable tank. See Chapter 10 for more on homemade cleaning supplies.

What's the best way to wash hard-surface floors? Start at the farthest corner in the room and wash them left to right until you wash yourself out of the room. Rinse your mop head or microfiber pad frequently to avoid streaking and dullness. Use your favorite tools and floor cleaning products and work as quickly as you can to wash your floors. Working quickly and efficiently you'll find that you're able to get this often dreaded task done weekly. If you find that washing the floors weekly is a little hard for you to keep up with, you can tackle one section of the house one week and another section of the house the next week. For instance, bathrooms one week and the kitchen or first floor one week and second floor the next. Don't be afraid to experiment to see what works with your schedule and cleaning style.

 QUICK TIP: If you use a washable microfiber mop head or pad, dampen it first with warm water. The water will help it glide on your floors, making it easier to use and it will get your floors clean more quickly.

Friday — Catch-all Day

I use Fridays to get caught up on uncompleted tasks, menu planning, bill paying, laundry, a rotating cleaning task, or if I'm caught up, I reward myself by taking the day off. Think of Friday as a day to get caught up with any tasks and to start the weekend with a clean house. You'll find that the weekend is so much more enjoyable if you're truly relaxing and not thinking about any nagging chores and cleaning that you "should" be doing.

QUICK TIP: If you decide to do your grocery shopping on Fridays, take a minute to wipe inside the refrigerator before you leave. Straighten out the shelves and make your list. The refrigerator will be ready to be fully stocked.

Saturday — Sheets and Towels Day

Saturday is sheets and towels day. Doing a couple loads of sheets and towels on Saturdays helps in the laundry organization department. Wash a load or two of towels and one or two loads of sheets. I find that if I start right away in the morning, by early afternoon clean sheets are on the beds and clean towels are folded and put away. It isn't a nonstop Saturday of laundry, I just tend to the laundry when it needs to be switched from the washer to dryer and then from the dryer to folded and put away.

 QUICK TIP: Simplify towels and sheets by purchasing white. You can wash them all together and on hot without worrying about fading towels and sheets. Use a scoop of powdered bleach alternative to keep them from getting dingy.

Sunday — Daily Cleaning Tasks

Sunday is a day of rest at our house, and I love that there aren't any cleaning chores to complete. I do daily tasks — make beds, check floors, wipe counters, declutter, and do one load of laundry and a little planning for the upcoming week, but that's it. Take a well-deserved break and enjoy your Sunday — do things that relax you and make you happy. After a leisurely weekend, you'll feel refreshed and ready for the week ahead.

QUICK TIP: If you are overwhelmed by the week ahead, spend some time Sunday afternoon or evening prepping food for snacks and lunches; jot down some notes and to-dos in your planner and you'll feel prepared for the week.

WEEKLY CLEANING TASKS CHECKLIST			
	✓		✓
Monday — Bathroom cleaning day		Monday — Bathroom cleaning day	
Tuesday — Dusting day		Tuesday— Dusting day	
Wednesday — Vacuuming day		Wednesday — Vacuuming day	
Thursday — Floor washing day		Thursday — Floor washing day	
Friday — Catch-all day		Friday — Catch-all day	
Saturday — Sheets + towels day	✓	Saturday — Sheets + towels day	
Sunday — Daily cleaning tasks		Sunday — Daily cleaning tasks	

WEEKLY CLEANING TASKS CHECKLIST

	✓		✓
Monday — Bathroom cleaning day		Monday — Bathroom cleaning day	
Tuesday — Dusting day		Tuesday — Dusting day	
Wednesday — Vacuuming day		Wednesday — Vacuuming day	
Thursday — Floor washing day		Thursday — Floor washing day	
Friday — Catch-all day		Friday — Catch-all day	
Saturday — Sheets + towels day		Saturday — Sheets + towels day	
Sunday — Daily cleaning tasks		Sunday — Daily cleaning tasks	

WEEKLY CLEANING TASKS CHECKLIST			
	✓		✓
Monday — Bathroom cleaning day		Monday — Bathroom cleaning day	
Tuesday — Dusting day		Tuesday — Dusting day	
Wednesday — Vacuuming day		Wednesday — Vacuuming day	
Thursday — Floor washing day		Thursday — Floor washing day	
Friday — Catch-all day		Friday — Catch-all day	
Saturday — Sheets + towels day		Saturday — Sheets + towels day	
Sunday — Daily cleaning tasks		Sunday — Daily cleaning tasks	

WEEKLY CLEANING TASKS CHECKLIST

	✓		✓
Monday — Bathroom cleaning day		Monday — Bathroom cleaning day	
Tuesday — Dusting day		Tuesday — Dusting day	
Wednesday — Vacuuming day		Wednesday — Vacuuming day	
Thursday — Floor washing day		Thursday — Floor washing day	
Friday — Catch-all day		Friday — Catch-all day	
Saturday — Sheets + towels day		Saturday — Sheets + towels day	
Sunday — Daily cleaning tasks		Sunday — Daily cleaning tasks	

Daily and weekly tasks will undoubtedly keep your home clean most of the time, but chances are you'll find that there are some other tasks like washing windows and cleaning appliances that need to be completed as well. After a month or two or three of doing the daily and weekly tasks and completing the challenges, start to add in the rotating tasks. You can do these in a day or two a week — they're meant to be added when you're able to complete them. If you aren't able to complete them monthly, I recommend doing seasonal cleaning checklists quarterly to get the same tasks accomplished. We'll talk more about rotating cleaning tasks in Chapter 5.

Now that you have an overview of the Simply Clean method, it's time to get started!

THE SIMPLY CLEAN METHOD — DAILY, WEEKLY, AND ROTATING TASKS REFERENCE CHECKLIST

Daily

Completed daily, these tasks are the secret to keeping your home tidy most of the time

❏ **Make beds** — make your bed and teach the others in your home to make their beds, too
❏ **Check floors** — sweep/vacuum as needed with a broom, vacuum, or microfiber floor duster
❏ **Wipe counters** — wipe kitchen counters down after meals and check bathroom counters
❏ **Declutter** — pick up clutter during the day and in the evening
❏ **Do laundry** — complete one load of laundry from start to finish every day

Weekly
The weekly tasks rotate through the week. Complete as quickly as possible, aiming for 10 minutes. Complete anything lingering on Friday or the next week.
❏ **Monday** — Bathroom cleaning day ❏ **Tuesday** — Dusting day ❏ **Wednesday** — Vacuuming day ❏ **Thursday** — Floor washing day ❏ **Friday** — Catch-all day ❏ **Saturday** — Sheets + towels day ❏ **Sunday** — Daily cleaning tasks

Monthly/Rotating
The monthly/rotating tasks are completed on a monthly, bimonthly, and quarterly basis. Follow the Monthly/Rotating Cleaning Tasks Checklist — for what tasks to complete and when to complete them.
❏ **Vacuum baseboards** — use your nozzle or brush attachment ❏ **Wash baseboards** — wipe thoroughly ❏ **Clean light fixtures** — tackle one room/ area a month ❏ **Wash rugs** — wash bathroom and area rugs

- ❏ **Clean oven** — use self-clean feature on oven or wipe out
- ❏ **Clean refrigerator + freezer** — remove food and wipe thoroughly
- ❏ **Clean appliances** — clean your household appliances (dishwasher, washer + dryer, etc.)
- ❏ **Polish wood furniture** — give your furniture a little extra clean and polish
- ❏ **Spot-clean walls** — wipe away any marks and handprints
- ❏ **Spot-clean furniture** — treat any spots and stains
- ❏ **Rotate/vacuum mattresses** — give your mattresses a little turn and clean
- ❏ **Launder bedding** — wash quilts, duvet covers, pillows
- ❏ **Clean window treatments** — vacuum, wipe, and/or launder any window treatments
- ❏ **Wash windows** — clean inside and out
- ❏ **Replace filters** — furnace, humidifier, dehumidifier, air cleaner, etc.
- ❏ **Wipe switches/phone/remotes** — give those most-touched areas a quick clean

CHAPTER TWO:
HOW TO PUT TOGETHER A CUTE CLEANING CADDY THAT MAKES YOU ACTUALLY *WANT* TO CLEAN

If you're on board with cleaning a little bit every day (of course you are!) you need to have your supplies accessible and ready to use. I've found that the best way to do this is to have a few cleaning caddies strategically placed throughout the house. If you're going to the trouble of putting together cleaning caddies, be sure to use products that you actually enjoy. It might sound silly, but purchasing supplies in your favorite color scheme *might* make grabbing that caddy a little more fun. If color coordination isn't what gets your cleaning juices flowing, make sure you're using quality supplies that will last. Trust me, you'll spend a lot less money if you use good supplies from the start. For me, less is more when it comes to cleaning supplies. Let's keep it simple and delve into a couple things you need to get started.

Cleaning doesn't have to be complicated and the supplies you use shouldn't be, either. If you feel like all the sprays and potions down that cleaning aisle are what you need to get started, resist the urge and stick with just a few supplies — you'll be glad you did!

SIMPLE CLEANING SUPPLIES EVERY HOUSE NEEDS

- **Dish or castile (vegetable-based) soap** — What your mom or grandma told you is true! A little elbow grease, soap, and water can clean just about everything!
- **Baking soda** — You have it in your house already. Don't be afraid to use it with a little water or soap for scrubbing action or sprinkle it in a garbage can to deodorize the stink.
- **White vinegar** — It isn't just for pickles! It has disinfecting and cleaning properties, and you'll want to harness this thrifty cleaning ingredient.
- **All-purpose cleaner** — If you mix up your own or purchase from the store, find a favorite all-purpose cleaner and

use it for everything from counters to floors.

- **Disinfecting cleaner** — I don't believe that every square inch of a home needs to be disinfected, but bathrooms and kitchens need a little disinfecting action. Find one that you can use in a variety of circumstances and use as needed.

- **Cleaning wipes** — There are times when cleaning wipes are handy. If you feel the need for a good cleaning wipe from time to time, stick a container in your caddy.

- **Furniture cleaner** — Polish, spray, or oil: you might want all three or maybe just one. Surprisingly, microfiber cleaning cloths and dusting wands (also on this list) can take care of your dusting needs in a hurry.

- **Microfiber cleaning cloths** — These little miracle workers changed how I clean my home. I love them for bathrooms, mirrors, dusting, windows. You name it, a microfiber cloth can clean it. Use them wet, damp, or dry for the ultimate clean. A wet or damp microfiber cloth works best in bathrooms and for counters and a dry microfiber cloth is great for dusting.

- **Sponges** — Keep a stash of regular sponges and erasing sponges on hand. They work great for simple counter wiping and for those tough-to-clean areas like bathrooms and tubs and showers.
- **Scrub brushes** — If you have grout and you don't have a scrub brush, go buy one now. I suggest a scrub brush just for the kitchen sink, a larger surface brush for bathrooms, and a smaller grout brush.
- **Squeegee** — I'm just going to go out on a limb and say you probably don't think you need a squeegee, but if you have glass shower doors, you do. I recommend a window-specific squeegee as well if you wash your own windows.
- **Dusting wand** — A microfiber head that's removable and washable is pretty much the greatest invention. It'll last forever and you know when it's clean. Shake out between uses and launder as needed. If you use a traditional dusting wand, like a feather or lambs wool duster, shake excess dust out between uses and while dusting.
- **Mop** — Oh, the mop. So many choices and surfaces, so little time! Whether a traditional mop and bucket, a refillable

spray mop, or a steam mop, the main thing that you need is one that works and you enjoy using.

- **Vacuum cleaner** — You probably have one, and if it has attachments, use them — they make cleaning easier.
- **Toilet brush** — I'm not a big fan of the traditional toilet brush; I prefer disposable scrub brushes. Whatever your preferred product is, use it — your toilet will thank you.
- **Bucket** — Some cleaning jobs call for a bucket. You might need to fill it with floor cleaner, all-purpose cleaner, or just soap and water. Keep a bucket on hand for those larger cleaning projects.
- **Caddy or tote** — Where should you keep all those supplies? Look for a caddy, tote, or bucket with a handle and stash your must-haves in it for easy cleaning. Compartments will keep your supplies orderly and any bottles standing up. Look for a caddy that will easily fit in the space you intend to store it.

START WITH A BASIC, WHOLE-HOUSE CLEANING CADDY

If you only want to put together one cleaning caddy, your whole-house caddy is going to be your best friend. By simply corralling supplies in one place, you won't be wasting time looking for that dusting wand or cleaning spray. Keep your caddy in an accessible place so you can grab it and clean. If you just need a duster, grab the duster and go dust. When you're done with each supply or the whole caddy, put it back where it belongs. Refill as needed and launder any washable cloths. If you're following the Simply Clean method for cleaning, you'll find that you aren't pulling out everything all at once for overwhelming whole-house cleaning sessions. You'll be using one or two tools at a time and cleaning a little bit every day. If you have small children or pets, keep it out of their reach.

Bathroom Cleaning Caddy

The bathroom cleaning caddy is a must for me. It's the only way I can clean my bathrooms in 10–15 minutes. I highly recommend pulling one together and giving it a try for your bathroom cleaning day. Here's what you'll need:

- microfiber cloths, paper towels, or cleaning wipes — if you're using microfiber, you'll need one cloth for all your mirrors, one for each toilet, one for each sink, and a couple extras for tubs and showers

- scrubbing powder or abrasive cleaner
- glass and mirror cleaner
- disinfecting/bathroom cleaner
- scrub brush
- toilet cleaner and brush — I prefer a disposable toilet brush system
- empty container for dirty cloths or paper towels
- caddy or container to carry supplies from one bathroom to the next

QUICK TIP: If you have children who are old enough to play a little by themselves in the bathtub, keep a caddy in the bathroom and clean it while they're content and playing. Make sure you use nontoxic cleaners if they're with you and of course wait until they're out of the bathtub to clean it!

DUSTING CADDY

If you are ready to jump on the cleaning caddy bandwagon, I recommend putting together a caddy with dusting and furniture care supplies in it. This will keep everything accessible and ready to use, which will save time and clear those dust bunnies in a hurry. See a scratch on your dining room table while you're dusting? Grab a furniture marker and touch it up right away before you forget about it. Set yourself up for success by keeping your frequently used tools at the ready. In case you feel the need to up your dusting game, here are my essential dusting tools and supplies:

- microfiber or dusting cloth
- natural furniture polish and/or spray
- beeswax polish
- furniture oil and scratch cover
- furniture markers
- dusting wand
- caddy or container to store dusting and furniture care supplies

 QUICK TIP: Put felt rounds on the bottoms of your chair and furniture legs to keep them from scratching your floors. Keep extras in your dusting caddy and when you see one wearing out replace it.

SEASONAL CLEANING CADDY

I don't keep a seasonal cleaning caddy on hand, but when it's time to do a little spring or fall cleaning, I pull together the supplies I know I'll be using and put them in a caddy to make the seasonal cleaning a little easier. Here are some of my seasonal cleaning caddy musts:

- all-purpose cleaner
- dish or castile soap
- microfiber cleaning cloths
- bar mop towels or cotton cleaning cloths
- dusting wand
- vacuum cleaner with attachments
- mop
- carpet cleaner (optional)
- blind cleaner
- scrub brushes — large and small (or an old toothbrush)
- window squeegee
- lint roller
- garbage bags

Once you've pulled together some cleaning supplies, you're ready to start the Simply Clean method. You'll be on your way to a home that is always simply clean and you'll get back so much time!

QUICK TIP: Putting supplies together in a closet can be just as helpful as putting together a cleaning caddy. Make sure you're prepared to clean regularly and that you have your supplies ready to go. Choose a spot to safely store the bulk of your cleaning supplies — a hall closet, your laundry room, or a designated cleaning closet. Less is more — choose a few basic supplies that work for you and get ready to enjoy cleaning!

■■■■

PART TWO:
THE 7-DAY SIMPLY CLEAN KICK START:
10 MINUTES TO A HAPPIER, HEALTHIER HOME

■■■■

CHAPTER THREE: THE 7-DAY SIMPLY CLEAN KICK START

If you've come this far, you're ready to approach cleaning in a whole new way with a different mindset. The 7-Day Simply Clean Kick Start is designed to make you successful in a short amount of time. Quick success with minimal effort is really helpful when it comes to starting a new habit. You'll find that this kick start is similar to any new habit that you try to put into place. There will be moments when you want to quit, but with a little perseverance you'll find that it's worth it. Trust the process and follow along to the best of your ability. Any effort that you can put into it will most definitely pay off in the days, weeks, and months to come.

Decide on when you want to start the

7-Day Simply Clean Kick Start. I recommend starting over a weekend if that's when you are off work or are most likely to have a little extra time. If you feel like you have oodles of clutter, you might want to take two days and up to a week for decluttering. The main objective is to not become burned out with decluttering to the point of quitting the program, but a little decluttering is necessary to *really* clean. Don't be afraid to over- or under-declutter — even one bag donated to your favorite charity is a step in the right direction. I would hate for you to be so overwhelmed by clutter itself that you can't start the cleaning routine. If you feel like you still have an abundance of clutter, we'll tackle that daily after the 7-Day Simply Clean Kick Start. Take a deep breath, grab a garbage bag, and get started!

DAY 1: DECLUTTERING 101

Clutter is different for everyone. One person might be able to sit down to a meal with a table that holds the week's mail and a load of laundry without it bothering them, while another person has to have all those things put away before thinking about starting that meal. Most of us fall somewhere in between those extremes, and it may be what's holding you back from keeping your home clean most of time. I've found that a quick and painless challenge can be just the thing to move a person in the right direction!

We're going to begin the 7-Day Simply Clean Kick Start with a little decluttering. You might think that one day isn't enough to declutter, but I think you'll surprise yourself with how much you *can* get done in a very short period of time when you're ready to get started. Instead of telling you exactly what or how long you should declutter, I'm going to let you decide. My one suggestion would be to *get rid of the piles.* You don't need to remove the coffeepot and toaster from your kitchen counters, but deal with that heap of mail and get those dirty clothes off the floor. If you get to the end of Day 1 and are convinced that you need much more, check out the Whole-House Declutter Checklist on page 377 for help. Feel free to extend the decluttering if you need an extra day or two, but even one or two bags of clutter removed from your home is enough to move on to Day 2.

How to Declutter So You Can Really Clean

There are just a few things you need for a successful decluttering session:

- a predetermined block of time — if you have 10 minutes or a couple hours, get to work and make sure you are ready to work quickly and efficiently. If you only have a few minutes to declutter, you can still do the challenge! Do what you can with the time you have and you'll be further ahead than you were the day before.

- garbage bags or bins — you'll need at least four bags or containers for things that you'll come across as you're sorting and decluttering.
- a timer — always a great way to motivate yourself to work quickly, a timer is a great decluttering tool.
- something to listen to or something to watch — make your decluttering session mindless by putting on your favorite music, a podcast you've been waiting to listen to, or if you're sitting and going through something like pictures or a box of items, put on a show or movie to make it a little more enjoyable.

Toss, Donate/Sell, Relocate, Keep

I use these four simple categories for anything you're trying to declutter — toss, donate/sell, relocate, keep. Put everything you come across into one of these categories and keep moving until you've decluttered that cluttered surface.

1. **Toss:** Throw away garbage. If it's something that can be recycled, put it in the recycling bin.
2. **Donate/sell:** These are items that you know someone else can use. If you're looking for the tax deduction, make sure you get a receipt from your donation drop-off. Looking to off-load your items to a friend or family member? Set them aside and label them for the next time you see each other. Want to make some money from that item that you don't use? Try an online neighborhood group, a garage sale, a consignment shop, or an online resale shop. Try not to get distracted with selling items right now — worry about clearing the clutter first and then deal with items that you want to sell once you've completed the challenge.
3. **Relocate:** This box is for anything that is simply in the wrong spot. Put all of these items in the relocate bin, basket, or bag and return them to their proper spot when the decluttering session is over.
4. **Keep:** These are items that you are keeping in the same general vicinity that you found them. Put them back where they belong.

Tips for Keeping the Clutter Away

Once you've gone to the trouble of decluttering, you need to put a couple systems in place to keep the clutter away or your hard work and effort will be wasted. Simple methods put into practice will make a big difference, but don't be discouraged if it doesn't click right away. If you've been bothered by clutter but haven't taken the time to deal with it, it may take a little longer to sink in. Keep working at it and you'll be closer every day.

Donate basket or bin. Keep a basket, bin, or garbage bag in a logical spot in your home. If there's something that needs to be donated, toss it in the basket and when the basket is full, take a drive to your favorite donation spot and drop it off. This simple step of having a place for items that you're ready to part with is perfect for keeping the clutter away.

Daily decluttering. Decluttering isn't just for kick starts, it's something that should be done every day. Decluttering as you go is a much better method of keeping things tidy versus waiting until the mess is so overwhelming that you don't know where to start.

Take it out, put it away. This is such a simple concept in principle but it doesn't just happen automatically in any household — it takes some real focus and determination. A great way to put this into practice is to ease into mini cleanup sessions in your home. These can be for yourself and/or your family. Choose a specific time every day where a little spurt of tidying up for a couple minutes will work. I find that before or after meals is especially effective because then the mess isn't nearly as large as it can be in the evening when everyone is tired and ready to wind down and relax. Only take out one thing at a time, clean it up or put it away, and then take something else out. If this doesn't always work in your home (it doesn't always work in mine), try daily mini sessions. You might need to evaluate and reevaluate your clutter strategy as you continue, but just keep at it and you'll see progress.

 QUICK TIP: Turn mini cleaning sessions into a daily thing as you're working through the Simply Clean method. Turn on some music, set your timer for 5 minutes, and pick up and put away as many things as you can. Repeat once or twice daily.

DAY 2: BATHROOMS

If you have one bathroom or five, you're going to spend time today cleaning each and every one of them. Master this method — it's going to be your new favorite bathroom cleaning routine. It might take you a couple times to get into the groove, but you'll find that not only is this method efficient, it also will help you clean your bathrooms thoroughly. And a clean bathroom is a wonderful thing!

HOW TO CLEAN ALL YOUR BATHROOMS IN JUST 10–15 MINUTES

1 Gather your supplies. Grab that bathroom cleaning caddy you put together! You'll need cleaning cloths (microfiber ones work great), disinfecting/ bathroom cleaner, glass and window cleaner, scrubbing powder or abrasive cleaner, a scrub brush, toilet cleaner and brush, an empty container for dirty cloths or paper towels, and a caddy to carry supplies from one bathroom to the next.

2 Start with your mirrors. Spray a little window cleaner on your cloth or mirror and wipe clean. Wipe from the top left-hand corner to the top right-hand

corner and "Z" your way down to the bottom right-hand corner of the mirror. This method will help you clean your mirrors quickly and it will also ensure that you aren't leaving any streaks or spots.

3 Next, move on to your sink, toilet, and bathtub or shower and liberally spray with your favorite disinfecting cleaner. But don't wipe yet! It's important to give your cleaners a couple minutes to work. If the cleaner has dried when you come back, just give it a quick spritz and wipe clean. Next time spray a little more liberally so it stays wet until you come back to clean it.

4 Scrub the toilet. I prefer to use disposable or flushable toilet wipes because toilet brushes gross me out, but that's just me. Use your favorite toilet scrubber and quickly get the job done.

5 *Repeat* this process in the next bathroom. Clean the mirror, spray cleaner all over the sink, toilet (tank to floor), and tub or shower, and scrub the toilet.

6 Go back to the first bathroom and wipe the surfaces clean — use a separate cleaning cloth for each toilet, sink, and tub or shower to avoid cross-contamination.

7 Go to the next bathroom and repeat wiping everything down until you've cleaned each bathroom.

Phew! The first time you use this method will most likely take longer than 10–15 minutes, but if you keep up with the routine for a couple weeks you'll be buzzing through your bathrooms in no time.

 QUICK TIP: Don't vacuum or wash the floors in your bathroom(s) when you clean them — save that for when you vacuum floors and wash floors later in the week. This is time saving and more efficient over the course of the week. Focus on one task each day and you'll save time and energy. If you feel like you just have to wash them to feel like your bathroom is clean, and you have the time, by all means wash them.

DAY 3: DUSTING

If you feel like you could dust each and every day of the week and still find dust to be cleared, it's time to dust a little differently. Proactive and methodical dusting will cure your dusting woes, but first let's talk a bit about where the dust is coming from and what you can do to keep it away. Dust comes from carpet, bedding, pillows, furnaces, airborne particles form outside, vacuuming, etc. In order to keep it from always showing up on your surfaces, furniture, and electronics, you need to stay on top of the dust. A quick weekly dusting and vacuuming will take care of most of the dust, but follow along for some great tips on how to keep the dust away.

Before you get started, let's take care of a few maintenance tasks to keep the dust away a little longer. Make sure you have new/clean filters on your furnaces, air conditioners, humidifiers, dehumidifiers, and air cleaners. Filters do a great job of trapping dust and particles from the air and it's important to make sure you're changing them as often as necessary for your home systems.

After checking on and changing your filters, give your vents a quick once-over with your duster or vacuum cleaner's hose attachment. If you can't remember the last time you did this or if your vents look especially dirty, you might want to remove them from the wall and wash and dry them or vacuum them out, making sure you remove all the visible dust and dirt.

Once you've checked these maintenance items off your list, it's time to dust, dust, dust! Today's task is to dust your home thoroughly and extensively. Grab a duster and a microfiber cloth (or your favorite dusting tools). I find that microfiber does a great job grabbing and holding the dust without spreading it around. If you have more than one level in your home, start on the upper floor and dust from the top down. Working from the top down moves the dust to the floor instead of making more work for yourself by having to re-dust things you just dusted.

Dust all the flat surfaces, lifting up and removing items as you go. If you spot something that needs to be put elsewhere or tossed out, put it in a basket and deal with it later. Work quickly and eliminate distractions to complete this dusting adventure. Once you've conquered one room, move to the next, and so on. Finish on the main level of your home with a top-to-bottom, left-to-right approach. You can easily split the dusting up into two chunks of time and complete it in the morning and evening or just plug away and get it all done at once. Once you've finished dusting every nook and cranny in your home, do a little happy dance and know that dusting will never be that difficult again.

DAY 4: VACUUMING

Once you've thoroughly dusted your home, it's time to pick up any dust that settled on the floor and get all those corners and edges that you've been neglecting. Today we're going to vacuum the home completely. Before starting, do a quick declutter to make sure you have picked up anything on the floor that you don't want vacuumed up. Once you've done that, it's time to start vacuuming. If you think you're off the hook because you have hard-surface floors in your home, you're not — everything gets a thorough vacuuming today!

 QUICK TIPS: QUICK TIP: The next time you're in the market for a vacuum cleaner, look for one that has attachments and a HEPA filter. These two things will definitely help you as you're working to keep your home clean and tidy.

Start on the upper level of your home and at the room farthest away from the entry to that level. If your vacuum cleaner has attachments, put them to use and do a quick vacuuming of your baseboards and edges before you get started with floor or rug vacuuming. Start in the farthest corner of the room and vacuum your way out of the room from left to right. Once you've vacuumed in one direction, vacuum in the opposite direction. This might seem counterproductive or like too much work, but it's a great way to get embedded dirt, pet hair, dust, dander, and anything else that you want out of your carpet. This method will keep those vacuum lines evident and also let you see what you've already vacuumed. Embrace cleaning with a method — not only will it make you more efficient, it will keep you on task and focused. Do a thorough vacuuming in each room, taking care to vacuum edges and corners and under furniture as you are able. You'll find that doing a really good job as you get started will make vacuuming weekly much easier.

 QUICK TIP: Change your filter bag as soon as it's full. If you have a canister vacuum cleaner, empty the canister after each vacuuming or as soon as it's almost full. Clean your vacuum regularly to avoid spreading germs throughout the house. You can use rubbing alcohol on a cotton pad to clean the roller and base of your vacuum cleaner in a minute or two.

DAY 5: FLOOR WASHING

Once your floors are vacuumed and all those edges are clean, it's time to give them a little love. When you vacuumed thoroughly yesterday you prepped them for washing today. If you know that your baseboards could use a little love today as well, you can wash them right alongside the floors.

Today we're going to concentrate on washing all the hard-surface floors in your home. I'm guessing you have a favorite floor cleaner and floor tool — grab your favorites and get started! I have found that a couple methods work really well when it comes to floor washing. Every once in a while, the floors need an old-fashioned, hands-and-knees washing. Depending on the time you want to invest and if you prefer washing your floors this way, you might want to go all out today. If not, simply wash them with your favorite method and tools. Start at the back of each room, in the corner farthest away from the door, and wash from left to right, washing your way out of the room. Wash every single hard-surface floor, including the laundry room, bathrooms, entryway, and living areas. Washing floors is one of the most gratifying home-keeping tasks there is — don't you just love clean, shiny floors? Spend a little extra time for a deep cleaning. The hard work will be totally worth it!

DAY 6: CATCH-ALL DAY

My secret to a clean house most of the time? I always incorporate and plan for a day to catch up every single week. This is one of the secrets to a clean home. Build in a day that accounts for life's surprises, because you know they're going to happen. Someone will get sick, you'll be needed somewhere else, or maybe you just won't feel like cleaning bathrooms or vacuuming. I believe it's absolutely necessary to give yourself grace and *plan* for that list to have more on it than you can accomplish. If you didn't complete everything this week or left something out, go back and finish it up.

What can you catch up on today? Take the time to finish up anything that's looming, uncompleted, or just bugging you. If you were able to finish everything this week, do a quick cleanup and declutter. Grab a bag or basket and walk through your home picking up anything that's in a spot where it doesn't belong. Once you've gathered a bag or basket of clutter, return each item to its proper home, put it in a donate bin, or toss it out.

That pile of laundry staring you down? Take today to wash and fold everything and put it all away. Laundry in its incomplete state can be overwhelming and can definitely give your home a cluttered look and feel even if it's in a pile on the bedroom floor. Moving forward, I recommend that you do one load of laundry every day (especially if you have more than four people in your household), but first things first: you need to catch up on your laundry quickly. Enlist any help you can get from family members, especially if you are looking at a mountain of laundry. Use this technique when you get behind or if you'd prefer to do your laundry weekly instead of daily:

1 Gather all the laundry in the house and put the baskets or hampers within reach of the laundry room. My recommendation for order is adult clothes, kid clothes, bedding, towels, kitchen towels, and cleaning cloths and rags.

2 Line the baskets up in order of what's going in the washing machine first to last. Start with adult clothes — do one load of whites (on warm) and one load of darks (on cold) per adult. You could also combine these clothes into

one load and wash everything on cold. Next in line is the kids' laundry: one basket per child — no sorting, all of it goes in the same load on cold. Depending on how much laundry there is and your washer and dryer's capacity, you can combine these loads into one, but for sorting's sake it's probably easier to keep each child's clothes together as one load per child. Remember that even little ones can help fold clothes or just toss socks and undies in a drawer. You're laying the groundwork for later, and trust me, it *will* pay off.

3   After all the clothing has been washed, it's time for bedding. Start by stripping beds and washing sheets and pillowcases. Wash them and put them right back on the beds to save time by not having to fold and put them away. As you continue through the Simply Clean method you'll see that on Saturdays I wash, fold, and put away sheets and towels. This simple step is such a great one to stay on top of bedding and to get your home ready for the week ahead.

4   Once the bedding is done, move on to bath towels, hand towels, and bath mats. Wash and fold everything and put it away. Take the extra second or

two to make sure you're putting every-thing away neatly; it'll be worth it as you continue.

5 Finally, wash any kitchen towels and any cleaning cloths or rags. Fold these and put them away.

While each load is washing and drying, fold, hang, and put away each and every load as soon as it comes out of the dryer. Depending on the wash and dry time, this will most likely go on all day but it just takes minutes to fold and put away the clothing in between each load. If you can't finish it all up, put it off until the next day and finish it up before moving on. If you have a lot of laundry, feel free to divide this up into two days.

Once you have finished with all your washing, put your washer on a clean cycle or simply run it with the hottest water setting. Select the extra rinse option and add 3/4 cup of white vinegar *or* 3/4 cup non-chlorine bleach (not both!) to the bleach dispenser or to your washtub and fill it to its maximum level. Allow the cycle to run until it has com-pleted. Open the door and let the washer air-dry. If you have a front-loading or HE (high-efficiency) washing machine, you will want to keep it open in between loads to allow it to dry completely. This will keep it from smelling and it will keep mildew away.

Once you're all caught up, I suggest, again, doing a load or two of laundry every day. I'll show you how to take it from dirty to folded to put away even on busy weekdays. Don't worry about that quite yet, but know that I have a simple method to help you keep your laundry pile at a minimum in just minutes each day.

With your laundry done, you have officially completed the 7-Day Simply Clean Kick Start! I hope you feel like you have achieved a monumental goal, and even if you don't feel like your home is where you want it to be, you have started a simple and effective cleaning routine in just a week. At this point you can repeat this challenge for another week or two or just continue right on through to the 28-Day Simply Clean Challenge.

THE 7-DAY SIMPLY CLEAN KICK START CHECKLIST	
	✓
Day 1: Decluttering	
Day 2: Bathrooms	
Day 3: Dusting	
Day 4: Vacuuming	
Day 5: Floor washing	
Day 6: Catch-all day	
Day 7: Laundry	

■ ■ ■ ■

Part Three:
The 28-Day Simply Clean
Challenge: Turn the
Method into a Habit

■ ■ ■ ■

CHAPTER FOUR:
THE 28-DAY SIMPLY CLEAN CHALLENGE

Now that you have completed the 7-Day Simply Clean Kick Start, you're well on your way to establishing your cleaning routine. It's time to challenge yourself to take care of the messes and clutter spots that remain. Each week for 4 weeks we'll work on a different area of the home. With focused and very deliberate effort, you'll quickly see progress and be motivated to continue and complete the challenge.

Once you've gotten used to your weekly routine, it's time to layer in some additional cleaning and organizing. Cleaning will never be this difficult again — this is your chance to completely overhaul your home and set yourself up for success. The best part of this challenge is that it can be completed in minutes a day. I've broken everything down into simple, manageable tasks that you can complete alongside life. No need to clear your schedule, just follow along. After 28 days you will have built the habits needed to make cleaning effortless, so you never have to think about it again. Cleaning on autopilot — what a concept!

Through this challenge you'll see a checklist for each week with tips and tricks designed to help you keep going and move right through each room. Use it to clean and tidy up your house so it feels like a home: lived in and full of life, not spotless and like you can't sit down.

I will be the first one to tell you that if you miss a day or have to take a break, keep going and don't give up. There isn't a magic number for how long it takes you to complete the challenge. You might even complete the challenge before the 28 days are up. Your number one goal should be to work on the challenge for a little bit every day, stay in the specific home zones until you have completed the tasks, and move on when you are ready. Skipping items or not cleaning them completely won't help you out in the long run. Stay focused and keep moving until you have deep cleaned your home — the Simply Clean way!

First Things First

Before you jump into the challenge, let's make sure you're set up for success with a little prechallenge checklist:

- I completed the 7-Day Simply Clean Kick Start.
- My cleaning supplies and tools are ready to go.
- I have set aside at least 10–15 minutes a day to complete these tasks.
- I can't wait to see my home transformed!

The Basis for the 28-Day Simply Clean Challenge

You'll notice that the challenge is 28 days long, which is also 4 weeks. This is very deliberate — research says that it takes 3 weeks to form a new habit. This simple lifestyle and mind shift is going to give you time, organization, and a clean and tidy home most of the time. You already completed a kick start and if you're still in this with me, you're *this* close to turning this cleaning routine into something that feels like it comes naturally.

You'll notice that each week has 6 days with directed and specific tasks and one day to catch up. I recommend setting your timer for 10–15 minutes each day and getting as much done on that task as you can. If you want to work longer or until it's completed, by all means, continue! Alternatively, you can choose to complete the tasks all on one day of the week. Here's the catch — while you're doing the challenge, you should continue to complete the daily and weekly tasks. I know you can complete the challenge and I can't wait for you to get time and energy back for things that really matter. Stick with me — add these simple challenges to your daily and weekly routine and you'll see what a difference it can make. Better yet, it'll be easier to continue after the next 4 weeks — it's like a clean little gift to yourself.

Take a peek at the challenge checklists (page 119) and you'll see that there are two versions — one with just the challenge and one with the daily and weekly tasks right on there for you, too. If you need to complete the challenge all by its lonesome, you have that to refer to; if you want to complete the challenge with the daily and weekly tasks, zip through those right along with the challenge tasks all at once or during the day when it makes sense for your schedule. Ready for more? Here we go!

WEEK 1: KITCHEN

If your home is anything like mine, you spend a lot of time in the kitchen. Eating, cooking, homework, hanging out . . . a clean kitchen is a great precursor to what the rest of the house looks like. There is no magic spell that will clean your home for you, *but* if you get your kitchen cleaned up you'll be more motivated to continue. Get your timer, grab your supplies, and gear up!

Before each day or task, make sure you have any supplies necessary, set your timer for 10–15 minutes and work as quickly as you possibly can. If you run out of time, set the timer again and keep going or stop for the day and come back to anything unfinished on Day 7. The goal of setting the timer is to stay laser-focused on the task at hand. Feel free to put on your favorite podcast or playlist, but put away your phone and turn off the TV so you can focus.

Day 1: Clear and Clean Kitchen Counters

Quickly remove everything on your kitchen counters and put them temporarily on your kitchen table or another space nearby. This means removing the coffeemaker, toaster, utensil holder, and absolutely everything else on the counters. Once you have cleared counters, spray them liberally with your favorite counter cleaner and wipe clean or use a bowl filled with warm water and natural, plant-based dish soap and use a sponge or cloth to wipe them down. Once the counters are clean and dry, selectively return the items to your counters. If there's something that you don't use daily and you have extra space to store it, stash it away where it's still accessible but not out on the counters. If there is anything that you no longer love, need, or want out on the counters, either relocate it or donate to your favorite charity or someone that you know could use it. Take a look at your counters — take a picture with your cell phone if you need to — does it look uncluttered and efficient? Ready for the rest of the week? Keep those counters cleared off!

Day 2: Clean Small Appliances

Remove your small appliances one by one and clean them thoroughly. If you need some guidance on how to best clean them, check out Chapter 8; you'll find a simple guide for cleaning small appliances. What's a small appliance? Toaster, toaster oven, coffeemaker, rice maker, stand mixer . . . pretty much all those appliances that you pulled off your counters yesterday. Today, you're going to clean them. Run white vinegar through that coffeemaker, wipe off the flour from your stand mixer, dump out the crumbs (ew!) from your toaster. Wipe them off and put them back and if you're contemplating why you didn't donate one yesterday, go ahead and do that today.

Day 3: Purge and Clean Refrigerator and Freezer

Start with your refrigerator and empty it completely, tossing anything that should no longer be in there. That jar of tartar sauce from a couple months back? Yeah, you might want to just toss that out. Wipe your refrigerator clean, take out any drawers or containers that can be washed, and wash them. Make sure everything is dried thoroughly and then put your food back. If your food is going to be sitting out for longer than 10 minutes or so (it shouldn't be!) move faster or grab a cooler. Repeat with the freezer and pour yourself a beverage. Phew!

Day 4: Clean Oven and Wipe Appliance Fronts

Cleaning your oven shouldn't be difficult, but if you've neglected cleaning it for a while you might have a little bit of a challenge. You can clean it with a nontoxic cleaning paste (see Chapter 10) or if you have the self-cleaning option on your oven, run that function (it's going to be stinky, so make sure you have windows open and don't need the oven for a few hours). While that's running, wipe down the fronts of all your appliances with a microfiber cloth and your favorite appliance cleaner. Once the oven has cycled through its cleaning, let it cool and wipe out any burned food debris with a wet sponge or cleaning cloth. Wipe it down again and look at that shine! You may never cook again just to keep that oven looking so pristine.

Day 5: Clear and Clean Pantry or Food Storage Area

If you have a pantry, be thankful for it and then empty it out. If you don't have a pantry, concentrate on a food storage area — a cupboard or a drawer where you store food. Empty your pantry out completely, throwing away anything that has expired. If you have some food items that you are no longer interested in that have not expired, donate them to your local food bank. Once you've determined what will be returning to those shelves, group your items in logical ways to keep it organized. Keep baking items, canned goods, cereals, grains, and pastas all together so you can easily see at a glance what you have on hand and what you might need on your next grocery excursion.

Day 6: Empty, Declutter, and Clean at Least Two Drawers and Cupboards (or One of Each)

Choose two cupboards or drawers today to completely empty out. These can be your two worst offenders or just spaces that you'd like to tidy up. Completely empty them, one at a time. Toss anything you don't love or use and relocate anything that doesn't belong in that space. Wipe the space clean and put back the items that made the cut.

Day 7: Catch-all Day

If you have completed each and every task this week, do a quick tidy of the kitchen and get it ready for the next week. If you have any tasks that weren't completed, go back and quickly finish them up today. Jot down any tasks that you'd like to complete later on your Unfinished Tasks Checklist (page 379).

WEEK 2: LIVING SPACES

The living spaces in your home might be a formal living room or a family room or maybe you have both. Give them some love this week and you'll be relaxing in peace without that visual noise that clutter creates. If you can only tackle one living space but you have two, choose the space that gets the most traffic and take care of that this week. Work on the next space the next week — simply repeat the steps and then move on to Week 3 once your living spaces are completed. Don't forget to set your timer, grab your supplies, and move quickly to get your home tidied up in a hurry.

Day 8: Clear All Flat Surfaces

Grab a basket or bag and clear any items that don't belong on your flat surfaces. This includes books, magazines, mail, nail clippers, knickknacks, keys, etc. Return any errant items to their proper homes and do a quick dusting of the flat surfaces with a dusting wand or microfiber cloth. Look around and ask yourself if the living space needs any of the items to function or add interest. If the answer is yes, put them back. If the answer is no, put them in a donate bag or bin and bring them to your favorite donation spot the next time you make a trip.

Day 9: Dust Light Fixtures

Quickly dust the light fixtures and lamps in your living spaces. Use a lint roller on lampshades and a microfiber cloth or duster on any glass shades, fixtures, or lamps.

Day 10: Dust Corners, Vents, and Baseboards

Grab your vacuum cleaner with your hose and nozzle attached and vacuum those pesky dust magnets. If you don't have an attachment on your vacuum cleaner use a long-handled duster or any other dusting contraption you can come up with. A broom with a T-shirt secured over the bristles with a large rubber band will even work.

Day 11: Deep Vacuum — Edges and Under Furniture

When you're vacuuming today (if you're doing this on a Wednesday), do a better job than you usually do in your living areas. Move furniture, go over the carpet twice (one time in each direction), and use your tools to capture any extra dirt.

Day 12: Declutter and Clean Storage Areas

Have a clever storage spot for things? Empty and clean that space out today. Concealed toy storage is a great idea, but if it's been a while since it was emptied, dusted, and wiped clean, it's time. Choose one or two areas today to concentrate on and table the rest.

Day 13: Launder Throws, Pillows, and Blankets

All those pretty decorative items hanging out on your furniture are going to get a bath today. Check the tags and wash as instructed. If you have any items that cannot be laundered, toss them in a cool dryer for a couple minutes to fluff them up a bit and to remove any dust.

Day 14: Catch-all Day

If you have completed each and every task this week, do a quick tidy of your living spaces and get them ready for the next week. If you have any tasks that are not completed, go back and quickly finish them up today. Jot down any tasks that you'd like to complete later on your Unfinished Tasks Checklist.

WEEK 3: BATHROOMS

Grab your bathroom cleaning caddy (you made one, right?) and get ready to get those bathrooms cleaned and decluttered this week.

Day 15: Declutter All Surfaces

If you like to keep your makeup and toiletries on your counters you aren't going to like this challenge, but stick with me and you'll be glad you did. Simply declutter all the surfaces in your bathroom(s) today. Toss old items, recycle anything that should be recycled, and put away what can be put away. If you keep your bathroom surfaces as clear as possible it makes cleaning them weekly so much easier. You'll just have to do a quick spray and wipe and you'll be done.

Day 16: Dust Light Fixtures

Quickly dust the light fixtures and lamps in your bathrooms. Use a microfiber cloth or duster on any glass shades and fixtures.

Day 17: Vacuum Floors, Baseboards, and Vents

Vacuum the floors in your bathrooms. While you're doing this, use the hose attachment to get the dust off your baseboards and vents. This is a great, easy way to quickly clean your bathroom floors and you'll be prepping them for a thorough washing tomorrow.

Day 18: Wash Floors and Baseboards

Grab your favorite floor washing tool or get down on your hands and knees the old-fashioned way and wash your baseboards and floors. See Chapter 8 for my favorite methods for washing baseboards.

Day 19: Empty, Declutter, and Clean at Least Two Drawers or Cupboards (or One of Each)

Choose two cupboards or drawers today to completely empty out. These can be your two worst offenders or just spaces that you'd like to tidy up. Completely empty them, one at a time. Toss anything you don't love or use and relocate anything that doesn't belong in that space. Wipe the space clean and put back the items that made the cut.

Day 20: Take Inventory of Bathroom Linens — Donate, Toss, or Keep

Empty your linen storage space. Wipe this space clean and fold and return the items that made the keep pile. Put items back neatly and by type to keep it neat and tidy going forward. If you have tattered linens, consider donating to your local animal shelter.

Day 21: Catch-all Day

If you have completed each and every task this week, do a quick tidy of the bathrooms and get them ready for the next week. If you have any tasks that are not completed, go back and quickly finish them up today. Jot down any tasks that you'd like to complete later on your Unfinished Tasks Checklist.

You've made it to the final week in this 4-week challenge. You aren't going to stop now, are you? Let's get those bedrooms dusted and deep cleaned and then we can all sleep better! If you leave your bedrooms until last and frequently skip dusting them because no one sees them anyway, this is the week to catch up on that missed time and to clear those dust bunnies out from under the beds. Don't forget to set your timer, grab your tools, and you're going to need that vacuum cleaner this week, too. If you only want to tackle one bedroom, tackle yours and write down the other bedrooms in your home on your Unfinished Tasks Checklist.

Day 22: Declutter and Dust All Surfaces

Grab a basket or bag and clear any items that don't belong on nightstands and dressers. Put these items in the holding basket and look around the bedrooms. Return any errant items to their proper homes and do a quick dusting of the flat surfaces with a dusting wand or microfiber cloth. Look around and ask yourself if the bedroom needs any of the items to function or add interest. If the answer is yes, put them back. If the answer is no, put them in a donate bag or bin and bring them to your favorite donation spot the next time you make a trip.

Day 23: Thorough Vacuuming

When you're vacuuming today (if you're doing this on a Wednesday), do a better job than you usually do in your bedrooms. Move furniture, go over the carpet twice (one time in each direction), and use your tools to capture any extra dirt.

Day 24: Vacuum and Wash Baseboards

Use a hose attachment to quickly vacuum your baseboards. Once they're dust-free give them a quick wash if needed.

Day 25: Clean and Vacuum Under Beds

Grab those tissues, socks, and miscellaneous items hanging out under the beds and put them in their proper places or toss them out. Move anything that you can in order to vacuum under the beds to the best of your ability. Getting the dust under the beds will help keep your bedroom less dusty for longer and make the air you breathe when you sleep cleaner.

Day 26: Purge Any Unused/Unwanted Clothing

If you've been meaning to go through your clothes and assess what you should keep, today is the day. Start with your own and ruthlessly purge what you can — donate or sell the unwanted items and make your wardrobe what you want it to be. If you have extra time you can always help another family member out or get them in on the fun and have them assess their clothes right along with you.

Day 27: Wash Pillows and Bedding

Anything that's in the bedroom that *can* be washed should be washed today. Check the tags of your duvet covers, washable pillows, sheets, and throw blankets and wash as instructed. If you have any items that cannot be laundered, toss them in a cool dryer for a couple minutes to fluff them up a bit and to remove any dust.

Day 28: Catch-all Day

If you have completed each and every task this week, do a quick tidy of the bedrooms and get them ready for the next week. If you have any tasks that are not completed, go back and quickly finish them up today. Jot down any tasks that you'd like to complete later on your Unfinished Tasks Checklist.

Cue the music and pop open the champagne — you completed the 28-Day Simply

Clean Challenge! Imagine that confetti just popped out of this page and I yelled hooray. What you have completed is monumental. I hope you take a moment to recognize it. But before you move on or get too excited, let's talk about how you can keep this momentum rolling in the next weeks, months, and years.

THE 28-DAY SIMPLY CLEAN CHALLENGE CHECKLIST

	✓
WEEK 1: KITCHEN	
Day 1: Clear and clean kitchen counters	
Day 2: Clean small appliances	
Day 3: Purge and clean refrigerator and freezer	
Day 4: Clean oven and wipe appliance fronts	
Day 5: Clear and clean pantry or food storage area	
Day 6: Empty, declutter, and clean at least two drawers and cupboards (or one of each)	
Day 7: Catch-all day	

THE 28-DAY SIMPLY CLEAN CHALLENGE CHECKLIST

WEEK 2: LIVING SPACES	
Day 8: Clear all flat surfaces	
Day 9: Dust light fixtures	
Day 10: Dust corners, vents, and baseboards	
Day 11: Deep vacuum — vacuum edges and under furniture	
Day 12: Declutter and clean storage areas	
Day 13: Launder throws, pillows, and blankets	
Day 14: Catch-all day	
WEEK 3: BATHROOMS	
Day 15: Declutter all surfaces	
Day 16: Dust light fixtures	
Day 17: Vacuum floors, baseboards, and vents	
Day 18: Wash floors and baseboards	
Day 19: Empty, declutter, and clean at least two drawers or cupboards (or one of each)	
Day 20: Take inventory of bathroom linens — donate, toss, or keep	
Day 21: Catch-all day	

THE 28-DAY SIMPLY CLEAN CHALLENGE CHECKLIST

WEEK 4: BEDROOMS	
Day 22: Declutter and dust all surfaces	
Day 23: Thorough vacuuming	
Day 24: Vacuum and wash baseboards	
Day 25: Clean and vacuum under beds	
Day 26: Purge any unused/unwanted clothing	
Day 27: Wash pillows and bedding	
Day 28: Catch-all day	

THE 28-DAY SIMPLY CLEAN CHALLENGE + DAILY AND WEEKLY TASKS CHECKLIST

WEEK 1:
KITCHEN

Day 1: Clear and clean kitchen counters	Day 2: Clean small appliances
Sunday — Daily cleaning tasks	Monday — Bathroom cleaning day
❏ Make beds ❏ Check floors ❏ Wipe counters ❏ Declutter ❏ Do laundry	❏ Make beds ❏ Check floors ❏ Wipe counters ❏ Declutter ❏ Do laundry
Day 3: Purge and clean refrigerator and freezer	Day 4: Clean oven and wipe appliance fronts
Tuesday — Dusting day	Wednesday — Vacuuming day
❏ Make beds ❏ Check floors ❏ Wipe counters ❏ Declutter ❏ Do laundry	❏ Make beds ❏ Check floors ❏ Wipe counters ❏ Declutter ❏ Do laundry

Day 5: Clear and clean pantry or food storage area	Day 6: Empty, declutter, and clean at least two drawers and cupboards (or one of each)
Thursday — Floor washing day	Friday — Catch-all day
❑ Make beds ❑ Check floors ❑ Wipe counters ❑ Declutter ❑ Do laundry	❑ Make beds ❑ Check floors ❑ Wipe counters ❑ Declutter ❑ Do laundry
Day 7: Catch-all day	
Saturday — Sheets + towels day	
❑ Make beds ❑ Check floors ❑ Wipe counters ❑ Declutter ❑ Do laundry	

WEEK 2: LIVING SPACES	
Day 8: **Clear all flat** **surfaces**	**Day 9:** **Dust light fixtures**
Sunday — Daily cleaning tasks	Monday — Bathroom cleaning day
❏ Make beds ❏ Check floors ❏ Wipe counters ❏ Declutter ❏ Do laundry	❏ Make beds ❏ Check floors ❏ Wipe counters ❏ Declutter ❏ Do laundry
Day 10: **Dust corners,** **vents, and** **baseboards**	**Day 11:** **Deep vacuum —** **edges and under** **furniture**
Tuesday — Dusting day	Wednesday — Vacuuming day
❏ Make beds ❏ Check floors ❏ Wipe counters ❏ Declutter ❏ Do laundry	❏ Make beds ❏ Check floors ❏ Wipe counters ❏ Declutter ❏ Do laundry

Day 12: Declutter and clean storage areas	Day 13: Launder throws, pillows, and blankets
Thursday — Floor washing day	Friday — Catch-all day
❏ Make beds ❏ Check floors ❏ Wipe counters ❏ Declutter ❏ Do laundry	❏ Make beds ❏ Check floors ❏ Wipe counters ❏ Declutter ❏ Do laundry
Day 14: Catch-all day	
Saturday — Sheets + towels day	
❏ Make beds ❏ Check floors ❏ Wipe counters ❏ Declutter ❏ Do laundry	

WEEK 3: BATHROOMS	
Day 15: Declutter all surfaces	**Day 16: Dust light fixtures**
Sunday — Daily cleaning tasks	Monday — Bathroom cleaning day
❏ Make beds ❏ Check floors ❏ Wipe counters ❏ Declutter ❏ Do laundry	❏ Make beds ❏ Check floors ❏ Wipe counters ❏ Declutter ❏ Do laundry
Day 17: Vacuum floors, baseboards, and vents	**Day 18: Wash floors and baseboards**
Tuesday — Dusting day	Wednesday — Vacuuming day
❏ Make beds ❏ Check floors ❏ Wipe counters ❏ Declutter ❏ Do laundry	❏ Make beds ❏ Check floors ❏ Wipe counters ❏ Declutter ❏ Do laundry

Day 19: Empty, declutter, and clean at least two drawers or cupboards (or one of each)	Day 20: Take inventory of bathroom linens: donate, toss, or keep
Thursday — Floor washing day	Friday — Catch-all day
❏ Make beds ❏ Check floors ❏ Wipe counters ❏ Declutter ❏ Do laundry	❏ Make beds ❏ Check floors ❏ Wipe counters ❏ Declutter ❏ Do laundry

Day 21: Catch-all day	
Saturday — Sheets + towels day	
❏ Make beds ❏ Check floors ❏ Wipe counters ❏ Declutter ❏ Do laundry	

WEEK 4: BEDROOMS	
Day 22: **Declutter and dust** **all surfaces**	**Day 23:** **Thorough** **vacuuming**
Sunday — Daily cleaning tasks	Monday — Bathroom cleaning day
❏ Make beds ❏ Check floors ❏ Wipe counters ❏ Declutter ❏ Do laundry	❏ Make beds ❏ Check floors ❏ Wipe counters ❏ Declutter ❏ Do laundry
Day 24: **Vacuum and wash** **baseboards**	**Day 25:** **Clean and vacuum** **under beds**
Tuesday — Dusting day	Wednesday — Vacuuming day
❏ Make beds ❏ Check floors ❏ Wipe counters ❏ Declutter ❏ Do laundry	❏ Make beds ❏ Check floors ❏ Wipe counters ❏ Declutter ❏ Do laundry

Day 26: Purge any unused/ unwanted clothing	Day 27: Wash pillows and bedding
Thursday — Floor washing day	Friday — Catch-all day
❏ Make beds ❏ Check floors ❏ Wipe counters ❏ Declutter ❏ Do laundry	❏ Make beds ❏ Check floors ❏ Wipe counters ❏ Declutter ❏ Do laundry

Day 28: Catch-all day
Saturday — Sheets + towels day
❏ Make beds ❏ Check floors ❏ Wipe counters ❏ Declutter ❏ Do laundry

I Completed the Simply Clean Challenges! Now What?

Don't stop. That's my first and most important word of advice. If today is a Monday, you're going to clean bathrooms (because Monday is bathroom cleaning day). Then you're going to tackle a little clutter, do a load of laundry, wipe the counters, make your bed, and sweep up that mess from dinner. These tasks are going to be sprinkled throughout your day or maybe you'll accomplish them all at once after breakfast. Or maybe it's a bad day and you did only one load of laundry and didn't even touch a toilet brush. What are you going to do? You aren't going to worry about it. You're going to go to bed and wake up on Tuesday and dust (because Tuesday is dusting day) and you're going to try to get the daily tasks accomplished, and maybe on Friday (because it's catch-all day) you'll clean those bathrooms. But if you don't, there's always next Monday. Doesn't that feel good? No pressure, no unrealistic expectations, just a guide to follow, some simple directions, and a whole lot of grace. You can do this!

Once you feel like you have a grasp on how the Simply Clean method fits into your life and home, you will have a better understanding of what will work going forward.

Try the routine as-is for at least 3 weeks (because you're forming a few habits). Let it sink in and work for you and your schedule. If you were starting from a fairly clean and tidy home, you will see progress much more quickly. If you are coming from a more cluttered home without much of a routine, you will be glad you stuck with it for a little longer. If you feel like you need to step back a bit, just complete the daily tasks for a week or two and then add in the weekly tasks. It might take a while for you to get used to the structure, but I promise you it will be worth every minute when you aren't cleaning over the weekends or trying to figure out where to start in a messy room. You have all the tools you need to clean a little bit every day.

The daily and weekly cleaning tasks are the backbone of what you're going to clean every day from here on out. Keep moving forward and don't worry about what you don't accomplish. Focus on all those little things you're doing that are adding up to noticeable changes in your home and life. Now that you've completed the 7-Day Simply Clean Kick Start and the 28-Day Simply Clean Challenge, you're ready to turn the Simply Clean method into a workable routine that you complete daily. If you have any tasks written down on your Unfinished

Tasks Checklist, take a day or two to finish those up. You'll feel better knowing that you were able to complete them all.

■ ■ ■ ■

Part Four:
Customizing the Simply Clean Method for Your Life

■ ■ ■ ■

CHAPTER FIVE:
LAYERING IN ROTATING
CLEANING TASKS
AND MONTHLY FOCUS AREAS

Once you feel like you are ready to advance past the daily and weekly cleaning tasks, you're ready to add rotating cleaning tasks and monthly focus areas. Let me preface this by saying that these are *not* necessary, but some people find that having a specific focus area during the month is helpful in keeping on top of regular home cleaning and maintenance. The rotating cleaning tasks are just that — cleaning tasks that repeat and rotate monthly, bimonthly, quarterly, biannually, and semiannually. These are the tasks that I've found are necessary in keeping a clean house. I'm sure you can add even more and feel free to do that, but from experience, those extra tasks are usually done on an as-needed basis or when you walk past it and think, *Huh, I've never ever thought to clean the top/bottom/edge of _____ and that's pretty dirty. I'm going to quickly clean that now or tomorrow when I have a couple minutes.*

Those extra tasks and to-dos are fine, but I'm not adding them in because I don't necessarily think they need to be done on a rotation. I have found that once you have a solid handle on a cleaning routine it's so much easier to add in other cleaning tasks that need to be accomplished. You'll find that you won't be overwhelmed with the daily clutter and you can clean with ease.

Here's a little explanation and rundown of each of the rotating cleaning tasks in order of how often I recommend completing each one — you can also find them on the Monthly/Rotating Cleaning Tasks Checklist on page 145. When and if you want to add these additional tasks in, complete one or two a week or do them all in one day. It is up to you and your schedule. For the most painless approach, find a weekly cleaning task that they will fit with and add them in. For instance, if the task is to wash/fluff pillows and bedding, that makes sense to do when you're washing sheets on Saturday. Don't overcomplicate things by trying to push it into your schedule, just look for ways to incorporate the tasks into your daily routine. If you're reading this and it just makes you nervous or stressed out to add in more tasks, skip right over this chapter and come back to it when you're ready or want to do a more thorough cleaning.

 QUICK TIP: Know your limits and accept that not every project or to-do item will get done when you think it will and that's totally fine. Use the Unfinished Tasks Checklist to keep you on track.

MONTHLY/ROTATING CLEANING TASKS CHECKLIST

Monthly

Vacuum baseboards. No one likes a dirty baseboard — this is an easy task to add to your weekly vacuuming. You can even split it up and do part of the house or apartment one week with vacuuming and the other half the next week. Keep it simple.

Vacuum and spot-clean furniture. Check your furniture once a month for dirt, stains, and any debris that might be lurking. Run a lint roller over furniture, use a damp cloth, or use the upholstery attachment on your vacuum cleaner. Give your furniture a little extra love — it'll keep it looking great for longer.

Clean light fixtures. Rotate through your light fixtures so they get dusted and cleaned twice a year. You'll see that each month has a different room's light fixtures to tackle, to keep it simple. And, hey, no one likes to be gazing at someone through a dusty light fixture. Keep them clean!

Wash (or vacuum) rugs. Once a month either toss your floor mats in the washing machine or take them outside and give them a little extra beating to get that dirt out. Run your vacuum cleaner over them if that's the method you prefer.

Polish wood furniture. Tuesday is dusting day, but every month or so use your favorite dusting polish or spray and buff those beauties to a shine.

Wipe down appliances. Okay, I know some people might read this and think, *What? She only wipes down appliances once a month?* Let's be realistic and just say that if you're wiping down as you see little messes, you can go longer between cleaning the fronts of your appliances. Or if you aren't wiping them down as you need to or maybe should be, at least do it once a month. And if you have stainless steel appliances, check out my tips on page 243.

Bimonthly

Wipe switches, phones, and remotes. We clean because it's nice to live in an orderly home but we also clean because it keeps us healthy. Every other month, use a rubbing alcohol wipe or a little rubbing alcohol on a clean cloth or cotton facial pad and wipe it over your light switches, telephones, and remotes. Do this repeatedly if there's a bout of something going around your home.

Quarterly

Clean oven. Depending on how much you use your oven and what you're cooking in it, make sure you're wiping it out at least quarterly. If you happen to have a little baking mishap, wipe it up right away to make the cleaning less painful.

Spot-clean walls. If you have little hands (and feet?) that travel up and down your walls, this might be required more often, but take a barely damp white cloth and wipe it over any fingerprints, dirt, and other foreign marks on your walls. If you need to, do a little paint touch-up during this spot-cleaning session. Pour leftover paint in a glass jar with a tight lid. Label the lid and keep it in a cool, dark place. This will make touch-up easy and it will also free up storage space because you can get rid of those nearly empty cans of paint.

Wash baseboards. I love clean baseboards. Four times a year, add a little scrub to your floor washing routine and give those baseboards some love. If you have little ones, give them a package of baby wipes and let them help. If you have older kids, give them a pack of baby wipes if they're "bored" and need a little job to do. Enlist some help and this task will (almost) complete itself.

Semiannually

Change filters. Every home's appliances are different — follow the recommendations on your appliances to make sure you're changing any filters on your furnace, air cleaners, humidifiers, vacuum cleaners, etc. Semiannually is a good guideline — go ahead and make sure these are getting changed a couple times a year or as recommended.

Wash windows. There will be a house divided on this and some of you might say that you have never washed your windows. Windows should be washed twice a year — it's a seasonal thing. I have some great tips for washing windows (hello, squeegee) on page 269. And hey, if you want to, hire it out. If you do hire it out, you'll probably never wash your own windows again.

Wash/fluff pillows and bedding. Pillows and bedding need to be laundered regularly to keep the dust, dirt, dust mites, and all the other creepy crawlies away. Follow the directions on the tags and clean them accordingly. Check out the tutorial on page 260. Most pillows and bedding can be laundered in your washing machine and dryer — hooray! If your pillows don't unfold themselves when you fold them in half, it might be time to replace them. When they're clean, make sure you're putting a washable protector on those pillows. They'll last longer and you'll sleep better knowing you can clean that next time instead of the pillow.

Dust ceilings and corners. You know that spot where your walls meet the ceilings? Invest in a long-handled duster and take care of these spots a couple times a year. In a pinch you can attach an old T-shirt or cloth to the bristles of a broom to sneak into those corners.

Vacuum or wash vents. This task works well when you tag-team it with washing baseboards. Remove the vents if they're disgusting, or if they're just a little bit dusty simply run your vacuum cleaner's hose attachment over them or in a pinch, use your duster to dust the vents.

Annually

Vacuum lampshades. You'll notice that I rotate cleaning of light fixtures throughout the house. You can clean lampshades then as well but this task will get you to do an extra little check once a year. Use your vacuum's brush attachment (make sure it's clean first) or a lint roller. Next time you have company, turn the lights on and know that the lampshades are dust-free.

Vacuum garage. If you have a garage, vacuum or sweep it at least once a year. This will keep the dirt out of your house and it will just plain look better. If you don't have a mat at the door to your house from your garage, now would be a good time to grab one to help you keep that dirt outside your door.

QUICK TIP: If you have the extra space, add a shelf or cabinet for shoe storage if you want to keep shoes out of the house entirely. I keep the kids' sports shoes and winter boots on a shelf in the garage and their everyday shoes in the mudroom in baskets under a bench. The kids each have a basket for their shoes. My husband and I store our shoes in the mudroom closet on a shelf. As semi-minimalists, we each have three to five pairs of good shoes.

Vacuum basement/storage area. It might be neglected, but a little maintenance will keep those cobwebs and insects at bay. Use a vacuum specifically for these unfinished spaces, making sure you get in those nooks and crannies and go through that old box from high school while you're at it.

Clean refrigerator and freezer. Again I might get some flack from the cleaning police on this one, but with weekly maintenance and wiping down of surfaces in the refrigerator, I find that I only need to do a full empty and cleanout of the refrigerator and freezer once a year. Of course if it's needing more attention, it gets it, but this is a good rule of thumb for a thorough cleanout and defrosting session.

 QUICK TIP: Keep track of when you've completed your tasks with a simple checkmark in this book, or use a notebook to track your home tasks. A record of what you completed and when you completed it is so helpful and you'll feel more accomplished. Gold stars all around!

MONTHLY/ROTATING CLEANING TASKS CHECKLIST

Complete these monthly rotating cleaning tasks when it works for you and your schedule. The most efficient way to complete these tasks is to pair them with weekly cleaning tasks when you are able. If you're vacuuming on Wednesday, vacuum the baseboards at the same time. If you're washing floors on Thursday, wash your throw rugs as you're gathering them to wash the floors.

JANUARY

- ❏ Vacuum baseboards
- ❏ Vacuum + spot-clean furniture
- ❏ Clean light fixtures — kitchen
- ❏ Wash rugs
- ❏ Polish wood furniture
- ❏ Change filters
- ❏ Clean oven
- ❏ Wash windows — inside + out
- ❏ Wipe down appliances

FEBRUARY

- ❏ Vacuum baseboards
- ❏ Wash baseboards
- ❏ Vacuum + spot-clean furniture
- ❏ Clean light fixtures — living/dining rooms

- ❏ Wash rugs
- ❏ Polish wood furniture
- ❏ Wipe switches/phones/remotes
- ❏ Spot-clean walls
- ❏ Wipe down appliances

MARCH

- ❏ Vacuum baseboards
- ❏ Vacuum + spot-clean furniture
- ❏ Clean light fixtures — family room
- ❏ Wash rugs
- ❏ Polish wood furniture
- ❏ Dust ceilings and corners
- ❏ Wash/fluff pillows + bedding
- ❏ Turn/rotate/vacuum mattresses
- ❏ Wipe down appliances

APRIL

- ❏ Vacuum baseboards
- ❏ Vacuum + spot-clean furniture
- ❏ Clean light fixtures — bathrooms
- ❏ Wash rugs
- ❏ Polish wood furniture
- ❏ Clean oven
- ❏ Wipe switches/phones/remotes
- ❏ Launder draperies
- ❏ Wipe down appliances

MAY

- ❑ Vacuum baseboards
- ❑ Wash baseboards
- ❑ Vacuum + spot-clean furniture
- ❑ Clean light fixtures — main bedroom
- ❑ Wash rugs
- ❑ Polish wood furniture
- ❑ Clean window treatments
- ❑ Spot-clean walls
- ❑ Wipe down appliances

JUNE

- ❑ Vacuum baseboards
- ❑ Vacuum + spot-clean furniture
- ❑ Clean light fixtures — other bedrooms
- ❑ Wash rugs
- ❑ Polish wood furniture
- ❑ Change filters
- ❑ Clean oven
- ❑ Wash windows — inside + out
- ❑ Wipe down appliances

JULY

- ❑ Vacuum baseboards
- ❑ Vacuum + spot-clean furniture
- ❑ Clean light fixtures — kitchen
- ❑ Wash rugs
- ❑ Polish wood furniture
- ❑ Clean oven
- ❑ Dust ceilings and corners

- ❏ Clean refrigerator + freezer
- ❏ Wipe down appliances

AUGUST

- ❏ Vacuum baseboards
- ❏ Wash baseboards
- ❏ Vacuum + spot-clean furniture
- ❏ Clean light fixtures — living/dining rooms
- ❏ Wash rugs
- ❏ Polish wood furniture
- ❏ Wipe switches/phones/remotes
- ❏ Spot-clean walls
- ❏ Wipe down appliances

SEPTEMBER

- ❏ Vacuum baseboards
- ❏ Vacuum + spot-clean furniture
- ❏ Clean light fixtures — family room
- ❏ Wash rugs
- ❏ Polish wood furniture
- ❏ Clean window treatments
- ❏ Wash/fluff pillows + bedding
- ❏ Turn/rotate/vacuum mattresses
- ❏ Wipe down appliances

OCTOBER

- ❏ Vacuum baseboards
- ❏ Vacuum + spot-clean furniture
- ❏ Clean light fixtures — bathrooms
- ❏ Wash rugs

- ❏ Polish wood furniture
- ❏ Wipe switches/phones/remotes
- ❏ Vacuum garage
- ❏ Vacuum basement/storage area
- ❏ Wipe down appliances

NOVEMBER

- ❏ Vacuum baseboards
- ❏ Wash baseboards
- ❏ Vacuum + spot-clean furniture
- ❏ Clean light fixtures — main bedroom
- ❏ Wash rugs
- ❏ Polish wood furniture
- ❏ Dust ceilings and corners
- ❏ Spot-clean walls
- ❏ Wipe down appliances

DECEMBER

- ❏ Vacuum baseboards
- ❏ Vacuum + spot-clean furniture
- ❏ Clean light fixtures — other bedrooms
- ❏ Wash rugs
- ❏ Polish wood furniture
- ❏ Wipe switches/phones/remotes
- ❏ Spot-clean walls
- ❏ Wipe down appliances

If you want even more tasks to complete, or if you prefer to focus on rooms or areas to clean and organize, you'll most likely benefit from monthly focus areas. Each month has a room or general area as the focus, with a few steps that you can complete over the course of the month. They should be simple to complete and take around an hour or two of focused energy to get them done.

The monthly focus areas are structured seasonally. Complete these right along with the rotating tasks. If you don't start in January, that's okay! I'd suggest beginning with the monthly focus area that corresponds to the current calendar month. For example, if it's March, start with the March monthly focus areas (spring cleaning).

January (Month 1) — Whole-House Declutter

Harness that New Year resolution ambition and do a whole-house declutter. You'll find that once you've decluttered, cleaning is so much easier. After the holidays, a big cleanup and cleanout feels liberating and gets you ready for the new year. Follow the Whole-House Declutter Checklist on page 377 for a more detailed list. If you are starting this in a month other than January, treat it like your springboard to a clean and organized home.

- **Declutter** — do a whole-house quick declutter and gather at least three bags of stuff you can get rid of
- **Clean surfaces** — remove clutter from flat surfaces (counters, dressers, etc.)
- **Sort** — sort through any existing paper piles that are out on counters or surfaces
- **Mail** — deal with your mail situation and come up with a way to sort through mail daily so it doesn't pile up
- **Kitchen** — declutter counters, cabinets, and drawers
- **Bathroom(s)** — declutter counters, toiletries, cabinets, and drawers
- **Bedroom(s)** — declutter surfaces, linens, and clothing
- **Living areas** — declutter toys, storage, and flat surfaces
- **Other areas** — declutter attic, basement, garage, and/or storage areas

February (Month 2) — Kitchen

Keeping a clean kitchen is important for health and safety, and it's just so much more enjoyable to cook and entertain in a space that works efficiently and logically. Follow these simple steps to get your whole kitchen clean and organized once and for all.

Declutter — completely clear counters and wipe clean

Clean surfaces — wipe cabinet and drawer fronts

Deep clean — clean refrigerator, freezer, and oven

Food storage — clean pantry or food storage area — discard any expired food

Toss or donate — items that are no longer needed or wanted

Organize — group like items together

Contain — use pretty containers to make food and cooking supplies more attractive

Label — to make locating items easier and to unify the space

Scrub — scrub the kitchen sink

Clean most touched areas — wipe knobs, doors, and handles

March (Month 3) — Spring Cleaning

Spring cleaning season is quite possibly my favorite cleaning time of the year. In the midwestern United States, it's barely starting to feel like the end of winter is in sight, but it's the perfect time to keep the momentum from any New Year's cleaning going to get those winter cobwebs and dust bunnies cleared out for good. I use a combination of traditional spring cleaning tasks with logical spring cleaning tasks to create a simple and easy-to-follow spring cleaning plan. Some traditional spring cleaning tasks like washing walls or cleaning out the fireplace aren't necessary, but washing baseboards and windows fit in nicely with opening up the windows and airing out the house. Follow the Spring Cleaning Checklist for a more detailed list.

SPRING CLEANING CHECKLIST

Use this thorough checklist to spring clean your entire home in 31 tasks or days. Use it how it works for you and your schedule and you'll be opening the windows and letting in that fresh air in no time.

Get ready	✓
Declutter your cleaning supply storage	
Clean under bathroom and kitchen sinks	
Gather your tools — make a spring cleaning caddy	
Whole house	✓
Dust corners, edges, and ceilings with a long-handled duster	
Clean doors and doorknobs	
Clean light switches and switch plates	
Vacuum and wipe baseboards	
Wash hard surface floors	
Vacuum/clean floor and wall vents	
Dust ceiling fans and light fixtures	
Clean window blinds and window treatments	
Wash windows and clean window casings	

Deep clean/shampoo carpets	
Living areas	✓
Clean lamps and lampshades	
Launder pillows and throws and/or fluff them in the dryer	
Thoroughly dust all surfaces	
Vacuum under furniture	
Kitchen	✓
Empty and clean at least one cupboard and drawer	
Wash/wipe cupboard doors and drawers	
Clean refrigerator and freezer	
Clean oven, microwave, and dishwasher	
Clean small appliances	
Clean pantry/food storage area	
Scrub sink and faucet	
Bedrooms	✓
Clean lamps and lampshades	
Thoroughly dust all surfaces	
Clean and vacuum under beds	
Fluff and/or launder pillows, bedding, and blankets	

Bathrooms	✓
Thoroughly clean toilets, sinks, tubs, and showers	
Wash cupboard and drawer fronts	
Wash bath mats, rugs, window treatments, and shower curtains	

- **Declutter** — clear surfaces and lose anything you don't use or love
- **Clean surfaces** — dust and/or clean all surfaces
- **Light fixtures and lamps** — dust and/or clean all light fixtures, lamps, and shades
- **Window treatments** — dust and/or launder window treatments and blinds
- **Clean and fluff** — rotate/flip mattresses and clean pillows, blankets, and bedding
- **Clean floors** — thoroughly vacuum and wash all floors
- **Clean most-touched areas** — wipe handles, light switches, knobs, doors, remotes, and phones
- **Deep clean** — carpeted areas, windows, doors, and baseboards

April (Month 4) — Bathrooms

Now that your whole house is decluttered and all the spring cleaning is accomplished, it's time to focus on some bathroom deep cleaning. If you have more than one bathroom, this can also be a good time to work on deep cleaning the bathrooms that don't get used as frequently.

Declutter — clear bathroom surfaces of any unnecessary items

Clean — clean and wipe all surfaces (counters, toilets, showers, bathtubs)

Deep clean — vacuum and wash baseboards and floors

Dust — dust and clean light fixtures

Window treatments — dust and/or launder window treatments and blinds

Clean neglected areas — shower curtains and bath mats

Clean most-touched areas — wipe handles, knobs, doors, and switches/switch plates

Stock up — plan ahead and stock up on toilet paper, tissues, and toiletries

Practice — take it out, put it away with toiletries and any items on the counters

Ambience — add something special (fluffy white towels, a candle, container for cotton balls, etc.)

May (Month 5) — Garage or Basement

If you're like me, the thought of tackling those seldom used spaces is not appealing. But this is the month to gear up and get it clean and organized once and for all. If you don't have a garage or a basement, work on a storage area or closet that needs some love.

Declutter — clear surfaces and lose anything you don't use or love

Clean — dust and/or clean all surfaces

Sweep or vacuum — clean garage floor

Organize — put systems in place that will get your household through the summer

Wash vehicles — wash or take to be washed

Vacuum floors — thoroughly vacuum and clean vehicle floors

Clean most-touched areas — wipe handles, knobs, doors, switches/switch plates

Deep clean — wash vehicle windows, clean dashboard, empty trunk, etc.

June (Month 6) — Bedroom(s)

Start with one bedroom — I always suggest starting with the main or master bedroom — get it clean, and if you have time or want to, add an additional bedroom. Look for places that are rarely cleaned — under the beds, behind furniture, drawers, etc. Give your bedroom(s) a fresh start and you'll find that you are more relaxed at bedtime. Bonus points if you aren't moving clothes off the bed to go to sleep.

Declutter — clear surfaces and lose anything you don't use or love

Clean surfaces — dust and/or clean all surfaces

Evaluate — what is/isn't working — write it down and plan it out

Light fixtures and lamps — dust and clean all light fixtures, lamps, and shades in living areas

Clean and fluff — pillows, blankets, and bedding

Fresh start — thoroughly vacuum and/or wash floors

Relax — add items to encourage calm and relaxation. Make sure the bedside table(s) are cleaned off and add a book that's been on your list to read.

July (Month 7) — Organizing Systems

Take a little time to think through the systems in your home and come up with better ways to organize those spaces that get daily use. Look for mini systems that can be tweaked, like calendars, a homekeeping binder, shoe storage, mail storage, keys, backpacks, coats, etc. We have many systems in place in our homes that we don't even realize. Even a chair that is always holding clean clothes is a system. This is one of my favorite months because it's the perfect time to concentrate on those little things that add up to big success or failure depending on how they are or aren't working.

Declutter — clear surfaces and lose anything you don't use or love

Evaluate — look at methods and systems already in place

Find three trouble spots — write them down and commit to taking care of them

Something new — choose a new method or way of doing something to simplify your life

Perspective — ask a friend for ideas or take pictures to see your home in a new light

Supplies — shop the house for supplies to put your new systems in place

Set up your systems — show family members how to implement

Add on — once the first system is in place and working, add the next one

August (Month 8) — Closets

If you have previously embraced the mantra that out of sight is out of mind, chances are your closets need to be decluttered and cleaned this month. Tackle one, two, or all of your closets, but make sure you completely and thoroughly clean one out first

161

before starting on another one. And take it from me: make sure you have enough time set aside to put everything back unless you want clothes and stuff everywhere. If you get on a roll this month and are able to tackle more than one closet, or feel like you need more time, feel free to drag this into the next month. Month 9 is simple and can stretch over a week or two if you need the time. I always feel more accomplished when I can successfully complete a task or project.

Declutter — completely empty and clean the space

Clean surfaces — clean and wipe shelves and wash/vacuum the floor

Evaluate — what is/isn't working — write it down and plan it out

Toss or donate — items that are no longer needed, wanted, or don't fit

Organize — group like items together

Label — to make locating items easier and more uniform

Practice — take it out, put it away to keep it neat and tidy going forward

September (Month 9) — Entryway or Mudroom

Clean and clear the space that's used most often for coming in and going out of your home. This is either your entryway or mud-room — or if you have both and feel ambitious, tackle them both. Get it ready for the next season of outerwear and guests with a simple declutter and clean. If you want a fresh perspective, go outside and walk into this space the way a guest would. Is there a place to put a coat and shoes? Is it welcoming? Is it working or does it need a tweak or two?

Declutter — completely empty and clean the entryway (coat closet, bench, etc.)

Clean — clean and wipe shelves and wash/vacuum the floor and outside entry area

Evaluate — what is/isn't working — add storage and make sure you have a place to hang guests' coats

Organize and contain — group like items together

Practice — take it out, put it away to keep it neat and tidy going forward

Slipper basket — if you want to make your guests feel especially comfortable and keep shoes at the door, add a basket with socks or slippers for them to slip on upon arrival

Garment care kit — keep a lint roller, sweater shaver, and any garment care

items in a basket for any clothing mishaps

October (Month 10) — Laundry Room or Area

If you have a dedicated laundry room or laundry area, chances are you aren't in the habit
of cleaning it on a regular basis. Take a little
time to give it a deep clean and organization and you'll be more inclined to enjoy the
washing and folding process. Okay, maybe
that's an exaggeration, but at least you won't
be putting your basket on a sticky detergent
ring on the top of your washer. Don't have
a laundry room or area? Put your laundry
supplies in a cute basket or container to tote
your laundry in style.

Declutter — clear laundry room or laundry area of unnecessary items

Clean — clean and wipe any shelves or
drawers

Deep clean — washer and dryer

Evaluate — what is/isn't working

Toss or donate — items that are no longer needed or wanted

Organize — group like items together

Contain — use pretty containers to make
supplies more attractive

Label — to make locating items easier

and to unify the space

Practice — take it out, put it away, and do a load of laundry every day to keep it manageable

November (Month 11) — Living Areas

Those spaces that you rest and relax in can take a beating with daily use. Keeping them clean on a rotation is simple, and it can really ease you into a calmer feeling when you finally do get to sit down and relax at the end of the day. If you have more than one living area — like a living room and a family room — tag team the tasks. Declutter everything one day and clean surfaces on another day. This will be quicker because you'll be concentrating on one task at a time as you work through your living areas.

Declutter — clear surfaces and lose anything you don't use or love

Clean surfaces — dust and/or clean all surfaces

Light fixtures and lamps — dust and clean all light fixtures, lamps, and shades

Window treatments — dust and/or launder window treatments and blinds

Clean and fluff — pillows, blankets, and cushions

Fresh start — thoroughly vacuum and wash floors if necessary

Clean most-touched areas — wipe handles, knobs, doors, remotes, and phones

Ambience — add items to encourage family time and relaxation (games, books, pillows, a candle, etc.)

December (Month 12) — Office/Paperwork

In preparation for the new year, get some of those papers ready for the end of the year and the upcoming tax season. Or maybe you just want to finally get a handle on the paper trail that stares at you and gives you that overwhelmed feeling. Follow the Keep or Toss Checklist on page 381 for a more detailed list and instructions on what to keep and for how long to keep it.

Declutter — clear surfaces and lose anything you don't use or love

Evaluate — look at methods and systems already in place

Find three trouble spots — write them down and commit to taking care of them

Something new — choose a new method or way of doing something to simplify your paper situation

Shred, shred, shred — follow the Keep or Toss Checklist (page 381) for guidelines

Supplies — shop the house for supplies to put your new systems in place — check your current supplies first before you go out and get more stuff to bring into your organized space

Set up your systems — whether it's a new filing system or an attempt to go paperless, get something in place that will free you up from handling paper

Add on — once the first system is in place and working, add the next one

Once you've gone through these twelve monthly focus areas, your home will be so much easier to clean and keep clean. Deal with the clutter, push through the mess, and you'll have more time and energy to spend doing what really matters to you. You can repeat this year after year and it'll be easier each and every time, or you might just need to complete it once. There's always something to clean and organize and that's just life. Accept it, embrace it, and do the best you can in whatever time you have to complete it.

January:
Whole-House Declutter

Follow the **Whole-House Declutter Checklist** on page 377 for a more detailed list.

❏ **Declutter** — do a quick whole-house declutter and gather at least 3 bags you can get rid of

❏ **Clean surfaces** — remove clutter from flat surfaces (counters, dressers, etc.)

❏ **Sort** — sort through any existing paper piles that are out on counters or surfaces

❏ **Mail** — deal with your mail situation and come up with a way to sort through mail daily so it doesn't pile up

❏ **Kitchen** — declutter counters, cabinets, and drawers

❏ **Bathroom(s)** — declutter counters, toiletries, cabinets, and drawers

❏ **Bedroom(s)** — declutter surfaces, linens, and clothing

❏ **Living areas** — declutter toys, storage, and flat surfaces

❏ **Other areas** — declutter attic, basement, garage, and/or storage areas

February:
Kitchen

- ❑ **Declutter** — completely clear counters and wipe clean
- ❑ **Clean surfaces** — wipe cabinet and drawer fronts
- ❑ **Deep clean** — clean refrigerator, freezer, and oven
- ❑ **Food storage** — clean pantry or food storage area — discard any expired food
- ❑ **Toss or donate** — items that are no longer needed or wanted
- ❑ **Organize** — group like items together
- ❑ **Contain** — use pretty containers to make food and cooking supplies more attractive
- ❑ **Label** — to make locating items easier and to unify the space
- ❑ **Scrub** — scrub the kitchen sink
- ❑ **Clean most-touched areas** — wipe knobs, doors, and handles

March:
Spring Cleaning

Follow the **Spring Cleaning Checklist** on page 154 for a more detailed list.

- ❑ **Declutter** — clear surfaces and lose anything you don't use or love

- ❑ **Clean surfaces** — dust and/or clean all surfaces
- ❑ **Light fixtures and lamps** — dust and/or clean all light fixtures, lamps, and shades
- ❑ **Window treatments** — dust and/or launder window treatments and blinds
- ❑ **Clean + fluff** — rotate/flip mattresses and clean pillows, blankets, and bedding
- ❑ **Clean floors** — thoroughly vacuum and wash all floors
- ❑ **Clean most-touched areas** — wipe handles, light switches/switch plates, knobs, doors, remotes, and phones
- ❑ **Deep clean** — carpeted areas, wash windows, wash doors, and wash baseboards

April:
Bathrooms

- ❑ **Declutter** — clear bathroom surfaces of any unnecessary items
- ❑ **Clean** — clean and wipe all surfaces (counters, toilets, showers, bathtubs)
- ❑ **Deep clean** — vacuum and wash baseboards and floors
- ❑ **Dust** — dust and clean light fixtures
- ❑ **Window treatments** — dust and/or launder window treatments and blinds
- ❑ **Clean** — shower curtains and bath mats

- ❏ **Clean most-touched areas** — wipe handles, knobs, doors, and switches/switch plates
- ❏ **Stock up** — plan ahead and stock up on toilet paper, tissues, and toiletries
- ❏ **Practice** — take it out, put it away with toiletries and any items on the counters
- ❏ **Ambience** — add something special — new towels, a candle, container for cotton balls, etc.

May:
Garage or basement

- ❏ **Declutter** — clear surfaces and lose anything you don't use or love
- ❏ **Clean** — dust and/or clean all surfaces
- ❏ **Sweep or vacuum** — clean garage floor
- ❏ **Organize** — put systems in place that will get your household through the summer
- ❏ **Wash vehicles** — wash or take to be washed
- ❏ **Vacuum floors** — thoroughly vacuum and clean vehicle floors
- ❏ **Clean most-touched areas** — wipe handles, knobs, doors, and switches/switch plates
- ❏ **Deep clean** — wash vehicle windows, clean dashboard, empty trunk, etc.

June:
Bedroom(s)

- ❏ **Declutter** — clear surfaces and lose anything you don't use or love
- ❏ **Clean surfaces** — dust and/or clean all surfaces
- ❏ **Evaluate** — what is/isn't working — write it down and plan it out
- ❏ **Light fixtures and lamps** — dust and clean all light fixtures, lamps, and shades
- ❏ **Clean + fluff** — pillows, blankets, and bedding
- ❏ **Fresh start** — thoroughly vacuum and/or wash floors
- ❏ **Relax** — add items to encourage calm and relaxation. Make sure the bedside table(s) are cleaned off and add a book that's been on your list to read.

July:
Organizing Systems

- ❏ **Declutter** — clear surfaces and lose anything you don't use or love
- ❏ **Evaluate** — look at methods and systems already in place
- ❏ **Find 3 trouble spots** — write them down and commit to taking care of them

❏ **Something new** — choose a new method or way of doing something to simplify your life

❏ **Perspective** — ask a friend for ideas or take pictures to see it in a new light

❏ **Supplies** — shop the house for supplies to put your new systems in place

❏ **Set up your systems** — show family members how to implement

❏ **Add on** — once the first system is in place and working, add the next one

August: Closets

❏ **Declutter** — completely empty and clean the space

❏ **Clean surfaces** — clean and wipe shelves and wash/vacuum the floor

❏ **Evaluate** — what is/isn't working — write it down and plan it out

❏ **Toss or donate** — items that are no longer needed, wanted, or don't fit

❏ **Organize** — group like items together

❏ **Label** — to make locating items easier and more uniform

❏ **Practice** — take it out, put it away to keep it neat and tidy going forward

September:
Entryway or Mudroom

❑ **Declutter** — completely empty and clean the entryway (coat closet, bench, etc.)

❑ **Clean** — clean and wipe shelves and wash/vacuum the floor and outside entry area

❑ **Evaluate** — what is/isn't working — add storage and make sure you have a place to hang guests' coats

❑ **Organize + contain** — group like items together

❑ **Practice** — take it out, put it away

❑ **Slipper basket** — if you want to make your guests feel especially comfortable and keep shoes at the door, add a basket with socks or slippers for them to slip on upon arrival

❑ **Garment care kit** — keep a lint roller, sweater shaver, and any garment care items in a basket for any clothing mishaps

October:
Laundry Room or Area

❑ **Declutter** — clear laundry room or laundry area of unnecessary items

❑ **Clean** — clean and wipe any shelves or drawers

❑ **Deep clean** — washer and dryer

- ❏ **Evaluate** — what is/isn't working
- ❏ **Toss or donate** — items that are no longer needed or wanted
- ❏ **Organize** — group like items together
- ❏ **Contain** — use pretty containers to make supplies more attractive
- ❏ **Label** — to make locating items easier and to unify the space
- ❏ **Practice** — take it out, put it away, and do a load of laundry every day to keep it manageable

November: Living Areas

- ❏ **Declutter** — clear surfaces and lose anything you don't use or love
- ❏ **Clean surfaces** — dust and/or clean all surfaces
- ❏ **Light fixtures and lamps** — dust and clean all light fixtures, lamps, and shades
- ❏ **Window treatments** — dust and/or launder window treatments and blinds
- ❏ **Clean + fluff** — pillows, blankets, and cushions
- ❏ **Fresh start** — thoroughly vacuum and wash floors if necessary
- ❏ **Clean most-touched areas** — wipe handles, knobs, doors, remotes, and phones

❏ **Ambience** — add items to encourage family time and relaxation — games, books, pillows, a candle, etc.

December: Office/Paperwork

Follow the **Keep or Toss Checklist** on page 381 for a more detailed list.

❏ **Declutter** — clear surfaces and lose anything you don't use or love

❏ **Evaluate** — look at methods and systems already in place

❏ **Find 3 trouble spots** — write them down and commit to taking care of them

❏ **Something new** — choose a new method to simplify your paper situation

❏ **Shred, shred, shred** — follow the **Keep or Toss Checklist** on page 381 for guidelines

❏ **Supplies** — shop the house for supplies to put your new systems in place

❏ **Set up your systems** — whether it's a new filing system or an attempt to go paperless, get something in place that will cut down on paper

CHAPTER SIX:
TIPS FOR CUSTOMIZING THE SIMPLY CLEAN METHOD FOR DIFFERENT SCHEDULES

There are so many household variables when it comes to a cleaning routine. There's the size of the home, the size of the family, and the amount of time the person who does the cleaning is actually home. The Simply Clean method works no matter your circumstances because of these three things:

1 There are always 7 days in the week and 24 hours in the day.
2 You will never finish everything that can be done and that's okay!
3 Homekeeping can become methodical and rhythmic — you just need to know what to do, when to do it, and

the simplest and most effective way to accomplish it.

Relax, work at it, don't expect perfection, and you'll find success with the routine. I know this to be true and I am confident that you will find your rhythm. Read on for some tips to make it work for your unique situation.

WORKING OUTSIDE THE HOME

Chances are, if you work outside the home and get home late or leave early (or both!), you are positively exhausted, with no energy left to put a cleaning routine into place. I've been there and I totally get it. My best suggestion is to start with 5–10 minutes of quick cleaning or tidying before you leave for work and 5–10 minutes when you get home. Start with the daily tasks (make beds, check floors, wipe counters, declutter, do laundry) and work on completing them every day. If the daily tasks are overwhelming, just start with one task. A quick declutter, a sweep of the kitchen floor, or a quick wipe of the kitchen counters. Once you've implemented one daily task, add a new one every week and before you know it you'll have built a little routine into your schedule. After doing all the daily tasks for a month or so, and you feel like you've got a good handle on them, start adding the weekly cleaning tasks — Monday is bathroom cleaning day, Tuesday is dusting day, etc. Set a timer for 5–10 minutes and do what you can in that amount of time and forget the rest. Don't worry about what doesn't get done — flip your mindset and celebrate what *does* get done. Keep going and before long you'll have added the next step to your routine as well. If you feel like you can add more time, and get more accomplished, increase your time to 15–20 minutes every day.

If you work 12-hour shifts or an unpredictable schedule, you might need to double up tasks and tackle two or three on your days off so you truly don't have to do much on workdays. A cleaning routine can be accomplished with any schedule, but give yourself grace while you're trying to figure out what works best for you.

QUICK TIP: If you're having difficulty finding time to clean but you really want to make it work, work backward to meet your goal. Let's say you want to clean your entire kitchen this month. Break up the tasks you need to complete (maybe there are ten) and then divide that by days in the month. You can either say, *Okay, I'll complete one task every third day,* or *I'm going to get all these tasks done in ten days.* You can do it — it doesn't have to be perfect, just get it done!

WORKING FROM HOME

I can attest to the difficulty of trying to balance work with cleaning and caring for a home when it's also your office. These two worlds don't mesh easily without some finagling. The key for me is to keep them separate (though some mingling is unavoidable).

I'm more productive when I take mini breaks as I'm working. I'm not the only one who feels this way — studies show that taking breaks throughout the day can actually help you be more productive. Choose specific times to take homekeeping breaks and throw a load of laundry into the washing machine or unload the dishwasher. These little breaks will get your body moving and allow you to get more done during the day.

I find it most helpful to get my homekeeping tasks out of the way early in the day so they don't get pushed to the back burner. I am a procrastinator extraordinaire and actually do pretty well when I put things off to the last minute. I've found that this trait isn't all that helpful for keeping a neat and tidy house, so I just get it done right away and get on with the rest of the day. Find *your* time to clean. Do you get more accomplished by dividing tasks up throughout the day or are you more successful when you get it all done before you start working? Figure out what works best for you!

STAY-AT-HOME

Regardless of your reason for being at home during the day, you have your own set of potential complications. It's easier to do the cleaning because you're home, but it's also hard to figure out when to clean and there's probably a whole host of other things you could be doing instead. If you're home all day every day, especially with kids, you'll also run into the feeling that the house is in some form of chaos all day long. Not only is that feeling defeating, it might prevent you from doing any cleaning at all.

Reframe your thinking. You're home all day, and if you're putting away what you take out, you are doing some automatic cleaning. That is just what you need to put your cleaning on autopilot. There are lots of people who would love to be home all day, so embrace your gift and do your best with it!

Choose a time or a couple times during the day when you are home, set your timer for 10–15 minutes, put away distractions, and do a little cleaning. If you have children at home with you and they are still napping or resting, clean during that time. I prefer to use nap and rest time as a time to recharge by doing something quiet, by myself. If cleaning is cathartic and recharging for you, by all means, clean. I prefer to do cleaning right away in the morning to get it out of the way, but maybe you feel most productive at lunchtime. Carve out a little time every day for daily and weekly tasks and work to make them a habit with a natural occurrence and rhythm in your day.

GETTING OTHERS INVOLVED

If you have children, get them involved in homekeeping. It will make it easier for you in the short and the long run and you'll be teaching them life skills that they need. A couple things that work well at our house:

- Take out one activity at a time. As hard as it is, encourage cleaning up one thing before starting another. Keeping toys in bins or baskets is really helpful for quick and easy tidying.
- Clean up before mealtimes, naps, and bedtime. These anchors in the day can silently signal cleanup times. Simply encourage a little cleanup 5 minutes before food is on the table or before getting pajamas on. If kids are encouraged to do mini cleanup sessions throughout the day it's so much less overwhelming for them than cleaning up a mess from a week of play.
- Assign specific, age-appropriate tasks. Look for simple daily tasks that kids of all ages can complete with a little guidance — laundry, dusting, making beds, cleaning up after themselves, etc. Getting kids involved at a young age is essential. Don't wait until it's too late — you don't want to be nagging a teenager to clean the bathroom or teaching them how to do laundry the summer before they leave for college.

Teach simple tasks and increase the level of difficulty little by little with age and ability and you'll be raising children who know how to fold their laundry, pick up after themselves, unload a dishwasher, and clean a toilet. Isn't that a wonderful thought?

 QUICK TIP: Include even the littlest kiddos in cleaning — put together a mini cleaning caddy with a duster, broom, spray bottle, and cleaning cloth. Even toddlers like to pretend to do what you're doing. Pretty soon they'll be dusting right along with you!

If you're looking to get a spouse involved in the daily and weekly cleaning, divide and conquer tasks together. Look at a checklist and decide what you can each do to maintain the house together. If you hate cleaning bathrooms and your spouse doesn't mind, delegate that task out. Have a master checklist in a visible spot where you can work from it together. If your spouse is not interested or on board, realize that cleaning isn't everyone's forte and not everyone has the same tolerance level for messiness. Try to integrate tasks in a way that makes sense for your household. Most people aren't interested in cleaning house after a long day, so mixing in little mini sessions is helpful. If it's bathroom cleaning day and you have the energy for a quick session after dinner, divide and conquer and see how quickly you can clean those bathrooms together.

WHEN YOU HAVE A CLEANING SERVICE

You don't clean your house by yourself? Lucky you! If you have a weekly, biweekly, or monthly cleaning service, put them to work doing the things that you don't like to do. Bathrooms and washing floors not your forte? Have your service take care of the hard-to-clean areas or do the deep cleaning. If you've ever said that you have to clean for the cleaning lady, you know that there are some things that need to be cleaned in between their visits. Depending on how often your service comes and what they do, you'll need to figure out what you need to complete on your own. Start with the daily cleaning tasks and see what else needs attention.

If they are coming weekly, you'll most likely just need to keep up with the daily tasks; if they come biweekly or monthly, you'll need to do some of the weekly cleaning tasks — I'm guessing you'll be doing some quick cleaning in the bathrooms and vacuuming

185

for sure. A little alert: I have had dozens and dozens of emails from happy readers who have let their cleaners go after seeing how easy it is to keep a house clean when you do a little bit every day.

 QUICK TIP: Hire help when you need it — most cleaning services can do one-time cleanings or can schedule two to four cleanings without a long-term commitment. Perfect for after a surgery or during a particularly busy time in your life. Ask for help when you need it! Consider hiring people for specific jobs like window and carpet cleaning to make some of those larger and more time-consuming tasks a breeze.

■ ■ ■ ■

PART FIVE:
HOW TO CLEAN AND
ORGANIZE (JUST ABOUT)
ANYTHING

■ ■ ■ ■

CHAPTER SEVEN:
ROOM-BY-ROOM TIPS
TO ORGANIZE YOUR HOME

Are you itching to clean and organize that one spot that has been haunting you? This chapter will delve into how to organize your home to make cleaning easier.

Before we go into room and space specifics, let's cover a basic speed cleaning and speed organizing checklist — use these lists if you don't know where to start or what to do. These two simple lists will get you cleaning and organizing any space quickly and with ease.

HOW TO SPEED CLEAN ANY SPACE

Knowing a quick way to clean any space eliminates the guesswork, which in turn saves time and energy. Follow this formula if you have unexpected guests, need to clean a room quickly, or just don't know where to start.

Gather your supplies:
- cleaning caddy — if you don't have a cleaning caddy put together yet, what are you waiting for? Go back to page 69 and put together your tools.
- garbage bag for tossing junk
- basket for items that can be relocated elsewhere when you're done speed cleaning

Get started:
1. Set a timer. By now I hope you have embraced the timer and seen how it can help you speed up your cleaning. Set it for the amount of time you have — even if it's 5 minutes it will be helpful. If you want to quickly clean an entire room, 20 or 30 minutes is optimal.
2. Declutter. Start by collecting anything that can be tossed and throw it in the garbage bag. Items that need to be relocated can go in your basket. Once the room or area is clean, put the stuff where it belongs, or if you're trying to clean up before someone drops by, stash the basket — make sure you deal

with the stuff before you forget about it.

3 Wipe surfaces. Quickly spray hard surfaces (counters, toilets) and wipe clean with a microfiber cloth or paper towel. If you have a favorite cleaning wipe, skip the spray and just go straight to the wipe for an even quicker approach.

4 Dust if necessary. Use your favorite speed dusting tool and move quickly, dusting from top to bottom and left to right. This method will help you remember where you started and stopped cleaning or dusting and will eliminate extra work and steps from your routine.

5 Do a quick sweep or vacuum. Concentrate on high-traffic areas and visible dirt and get that cleaned up first before moving on to other areas. Because you are quick cleaning, a deep vacuuming isn't necessary — just concentrate on visible debris.

6 Straighten throw blankets and pillows. Take a minute to straighten up throw pillows and blankets. Give pillows a fluff and arrange them in a way that's visually pleasing to you. Straightening up pillows and blankets will give your room a completed and neat appearance even if it isn't perfectly clean.

7 Change towels. If you speed cleaned your kitchen or bathroom, put out fresh towels to complete the space. Fold hand towels in thirds the long way when you put them away so they are easy to hang on towel rings and bars.

 QUICK TIP: Get in the habit of wiping down kitchen counters after dinner and putting out fresh towels. This simple task will pay off the next morning when you wake up to a clean kitchen — it's much more enjoyable to drink that morning coffee or tea when you aren't staring down a messy counter. Think of these mini kitchen tasks as gifts to your future self.

How to Speed Organize Any Space

If you've ever felt completely overwhelmed opening up a closet or drawer, you need a speed organizing session. This method is most successful when you have a space that desperately needs a little organization and you only have a few minutes to get it in order. If you have an entire room or a closet to tackle, you can still follow these steps but it will take a little bit longer.

 QUICK TIP: Always completely empty any space you're trying to organize. Not only will you find that you are able to organize it more effectively, you're also less likely to put everything back if you're forced to deal with it, making it easier to really declutter.

Gather your supplies:
- garbage bag (for things that you want to toss)
- cleaning cloth
- all-purpose cleaner
- 4 containers to sort items in — toss, keep, relocate, donate. You can use laundry baskets, cardboard boxes, or any empty container to sort your items in.

Get started:
1 Completely empty the space. If it's a drawer or a cupboard, empty it all out onto the floor or a table nearby. Don't get distracted with what you just un-

earthed from your disorganized space. Stay on task and move on to the next step.

2 Wipe the area clean. If you're going to take the time to organize a space, take the time to clean the surfaces — it's worth it!

3 Sort. Quickly sort all the items into four piles — toss, donate/sell, relocate, keep. Use your garbage bag for the toss items, keep is for the items that will stay in the space, relocate is for anything that you still want but doesn't belong here, and donate is for items that you don't want but someone else can use.

4 Put away the keep pile. Once you have sorted through your space, it's time to put the keep pile away. Before you start putting everything back, take a minute to re-sort the items and put them into groups. The number one rule to an organized home is putting like items with like items. Pencils go in the pencil box, magazines go in the magazine basket, books go on the bookshelf, forks go with forks, etc. Keeping your items grouped together eliminates searching, which saves time and money when you're running a household.

5 Contain. Once you've organized your space, you might need a container or two to help you keep your space organized. Search your house for something you can use to organize. If you come up empty-handed, put a solution on your shopping list.

 QUICK TIP: Keep a donate basket or bag in your house — when the basket is filled up, take a drive to your local charity shop.

KITCHEN

The kitchen is often the most-used room in the home and it can also play host to more germs than any other room. Knowing how to organize it for efficiency and clean it for safety is essential, but what about those hard-to-clean spots like under the refrigerator and the greasy vent hood? Cleaning the kitchen on a schedule is important, but knowing how to clean pesky spots is also key to unlocking the mystery of a kitchen that stays clean *and* organized.

QUICK TIP: For smelly kitchen odors (like a fishy dinner smell that won't go away), pour 1/4–1/2 cup of white vinegar in a small bowl and let it sit uncovered on a counter for 24 hours. The vinegar will absorb the odor and leave your kitchen smelling neutral again.

Kitchen Speed Cleaning Checklist

You don't need to spend the day cleaning the kitchen to make it sparkle. This speed cleaning checklist will get your kitchen shining in no time.

QUICK TIP: This is a great little checklist to complete nightly after dinner. If you're starting with a semiclean kitchen you should be able to work through the list in about 15 minutes.

Keep your favorite kitchen cleaning tools and cleaners in a caddy or container under the kitchen sink so you can grab them and clean anytime. My must-have tools for a clean kitchen?

- kitchen sink scrub powder or gel
- scrub brush
- all-purpose and/or disinfecting cleaner
- stainless steel cleaner
- microfiber cloths
- bar mop towels to clean counters
- sponges
- dish soap — look for natural and plant-based varieties

KITCHEN SPEED CLEANING CHECKLIST	
Use this checklist for after-dinner cleanup or just as a reference for how to get this job done in a hurry.	
Set a timer — Eliminate any distractions and set a timer for 10–15 minutes.	
Quick declutter — Collect anything on the counters and kitchen table that doesn't belong. Don't worry about putting these items away right now.	
Unload/load dishwasher — If you have dishes on the counter or sink, load them in the empty dishwasher.	
Clean the sink — Give your sink a little scrub. You'll be amazed how this simple task can impact your kitchen cleanliness.	

Wipe surfaces — Spray counters and the kitchen table and wipe clean with a cloth or sponge. Once you're in the habit of wiping down counters daily, this is a simple and manageable task.	
Check the stove for any spills — If you see any spills or burned-on food, quickly wipe them away.	
Quick sweep or vacuum — Check under the table and in the corners for any crumbs that can be quickly swept up.	
Put out fresh hand and dish towels — The final touch to the clean kitchen is a fresh towel.	

 QUICK TIP: A lazy Susan makes a great under-the-kitchen-sink organizer — everything is easily accessible and any drips from the soaps or sprays are on the lazy Susan and not your cabinet.

Get started:

1 Set a timer. Setting a timer is a great way to motivate to clean quickly. Eliminate any distractions, set a timer for

10–15 minutes, and see how much you can get done.

2 Quick declutter. Collect anything on the counters and kitchen table that doesn't belong. Don't put these items away right now, but get them out of the kitchen, pronto.

3 Unload/load dishwasher. It only takes 3–4 minutes to unload a dishwasher and put the dishes away — stop putting it off and just do it! If you have dishes on the counter or sink, load them in the empty dishwasher.

4 Clean the sink. Give your sink a little scrub (see the recipe for my sink scrub on page 305) — you'll be amazed how this simple task can impact your kitchen cleanliness.

5 Wipe surfaces. Spray counters and the kitchen table and wipe clean with a cloth or sponge. Once you're in the habit of wiping down counters daily, this is a simple and manageable task.

6 Check the stove for any spills. If you see any spills or burned-on food, quickly wipe it away. If you don't have time and you have company at the door, place a teakettle over the spot to conceal it.

7 Quick sweep or vacuum. Check the floors for any visible dirt — if you spot

something, sweep or vacuum it up quickly.

8 Put out fresh towels. Put out fresh, clean towels as you're making your final check of the kitchen.

A kitchen that can be quickly cleaned will save you time, energy, and — if a dirty space bothers you — your sanity. If you want to do a kitchen deep clean go back to Week 1 of the Simply Clean Challenge (page 104) to clean your kitchen from top to bottom.

Organize a Kitchen for the Best Efficiency — Create Zones

Once your kitchen is consistently clean and you feel like you are ready to organize this hub of your home, the first thing you should do is to create zones. Zones will help you stay efficient in the kitchen by making it easier to locate common and seldom used items as well as giving everything a logical place. Here are the zones in my kitchen — these may or may not make sense for you and your needs but you can easily adjust and figure out what works.

1. **Dishwasher zone** — Think of ways that you can create easy access and put-away-ability to create an efficient

dishwasher zone. You should be able to stand in one general vicinity to empty and load the dishwasher, with dish soap, silverware, storage containers, dish towels, and dishes all within reach.

 QUICK TIP: Keep dishwasher detergent pods or powder in a large vintage canning jar on the counter above the dishwasher—this keeps them accessible and easy to grab.

2. **Baking zone** — Store baking supplies, flours and sugars, a mixer and/or stand mixer, spices, measuring cups and spoons, oils, and a cookbook holder in a cabinet or in multiple cabinets and drawers that are grouped together.
3. **Menu planning zone** — If you're a menu planner, keep the things you use frequently in one place. I keep my recipe binders, a handful of cookbooks, and a menu plan for the week/shopping list on a shelf in the kitchen. I can grab what I need and make a plan for the week in a couple minutes.
4. **Coffee and tea zone** — Store cups and mugs in the same area as your

coffeepot. Keep tea bags in a bowl or covered container so you can pull them out freely and offer guests (or yourself) choices.

 QUICK TIP: Limited counter space? Eliminate any rarely used small appliances and store the necessary appliances in a cupboard to free up counter space. Put appliances that you don't use daily or weekly away and get them off the counters. This will make it easier to keep the counters clean and it will give your kitchen a more uncluttered look and feel.

Tips and Tricks to Reduce Paper in the Kitchen

If you're looking to reduce paper product usage in the kitchen, you'll save money and it'll be better for the environment. Using cloth products eliminates the extra waste, but it can create a little more work in the laundry room. I've been using cloth products in the kitchen for years and have a couple tips to make it easier than you might anticipate.

Paper towels — If you want to stop using paper towels, just stop buying paper towels and put away your paper towel holder. As a replacement for paper towels, my recommendation is to buy at least a dozen bar mop cloths and put them in a container where your paper towels used to be. I use a lidded jar and roll up the bar mop towels — it looks nice and serves a purpose. Use one or two cloths every day when wiping down counters, surfaces, and tables.

Kitchen towels — Have kitchen towels that you love and keep them folded up in a convenient place or drawer to grab and use for hand drying. Put out fresh hand towels nightly so you have clean, fresh towels ready for the next day.

Microfiber — I use microfiber to wipe and clean appliances (microfiber will last through 300-plus washings). Keep a handful of microfiber cloths in the kitchen — I keep them in the drawer with bar mop towels.

Fabric napkins — Add fabric napkins if you're feeling ambitious. This is something that I tried, but I went back to paper when my youngest was a baby. We use fabric napkins occasionally but not daily.

Whether you eliminate all paper products or simply start using fewer, figure out the simplest way to organize the cloth so you use it and enjoy using it!

How to Organize Any Kitchen Drawer or Cabinet in Minutes

Organized drawers and cabinets are essential for any kitchen to operate smoothly. If you open a kitchen drawer and suddenly can't find the ice cream scoop you were looking for — or maybe you can't even open that drawer — it's time to do a little quick organizing. If you feel ambitious, choose your worst drawer or cabinet, or just choose a space that's been bugging you. Be warned: one organized kitchen drawer can lead you to a quest of organizing every kitchen drawer and cabinet.

Gather your supplies:
- garbage bag (for things that you want to toss)
- cleaning cloth
- all-purpose cleaner

Get started:
1 Completely empty the drawer or cabinet.
2 Spray with your favorite all-purpose

cleaner and wipe area clean.

3   Toss any items that cannot be donated or relocated to another space.

4   Move any items that can be placed in another, more logical space in the kitchen. If you have duplicates, donate the extras to save space and to simplify.

5   Group like items together. If you only follow one rule of organizing, this is the one when it comes to organizing drawers and cabinets. Keeping like items grouped together makes it easy to find items and even easier to put them away.

6   Drawer dividers and organizers are your friends — determine the correct size for your drawer and/or cabinet and the approximate number of compartments.

7   Label anything that needs to be labeled so items will be returned to their new home. It may be helpful to use a label maker to label the side or bottom of the compartments of any organizers. I added a label to the top of drawers and drawer organizers and, while I might not need it, my little helpers love using it to put away and find those often used kitchen items.

•   Return your items to your kitchen drawer or cabinet.

How to Organize a Pantry

An organized pantry can be blissful, but a little disorganization can quickly give you that overwhelmed feeling. I have a simple system for putting organization back into your pantry — with a little time and focus, you can experience food storage bliss, too. You'll be able to locate food quickly and you'll know precisely what you have on hand and what you need.

Gather your supplies:
- garbage bag (for things that you want to toss)
- cleaning cloth
- all-purpose cleaner
- sticky notes and pen

Get started:
1 Before you do anything, determine a couple zones that you can put everything into. Determine categories that work for how you cook and bake and what you store: snacks, cooking, baking, beverages, cereals, lunch supplies, food storage supplies, canned goods, grains and pastas, condiments, etc.
2 Write these zones down on sticky notes and place the notes on a kitchen table or counter where you will be grouping

items together.

3 Completely empty your pantry or food storage area and place items in their appropriate category on your kitchen table or counter.

4 Toss any expired food. If you have other food items that you no longer want or need that haven't expired, donate them to your local food bank.

5 Spray the food storage area with all-purpose cleaner (make sure it's non-toxic) and wipe with your cleaning cloth. Wipe up any spills and drips that you see. You can spray a little cleaner on your cloth and wipe that way as well.

6 Put your pantry or food storage into zones. Once you've set up your categories, place items back in a way that makes sense. If you have wire shelving, use short-sided plastic boxes to contain baking and cooking supplies. If you have solid shelves, indulge in lazy Susans — they will change your life. Both of these solutions allow you to see each item, and if the oil or vinegar drips or leaks, it stays inside the container and off the shelf below. If you love to bake and bake often, baking supplies should be front and center. If your kids pack

their own lunches or get their own snacks, put them where they are easily accessible.

7 Contain and label. The pantry is where labels and containers do their best work — they are definitely worth considering. You can purchase containers that come with their own labels or reuse glass canning jars with taped labels. I love using a white oil-based paint marker on glass jars to label the contents. It looks custom and will stay on through washing. I use a drop of lemon essential oil on a cotton pad when I want to remove the label. Easy-peasy. Think outside the box and inside your budget to come up with a solution that works for you!

 QUICK TIP: Have extra storage space? Purchase two of every condiment when you run out so you always have it on hand and can simplify grocery list making.

How to Maintain an Organized Pantry

It's one thing to get your pantry or food storage area all organized, but keeping it that way can be a challenge. Put these ideas in place for an accessible and organized pantry.

 QUICK TIP: Remove cooking instructions from boxes and bags and tape to the back of storage containers so you know how long to cook, say, 4 servings of long-grain rice.

Get started:

1 Have specific zones in place that make sense — baking supplies, cooking supplies, grains, snacks, etc. Label the zones permanently or temporarily if you're trying to get others on board with the new solution.

2 Remove products from their original packages to keep a uniform and more organized look in your pantry.

3 Take it out, put it away.

4 Take the time to put items away where they belong when you return from the grocery store.

QUICK TIP: If you're feeling extra-ambitious, keep a pantry inventory sheet to track what you have on hand and what you need. Make a list of must-have items and keep track of quantities.

How to Organize a Refrigerator

Having a clean and organized refrigerator can make such a big difference for both efficiency and peace of mind. You can label drawers, add bins and organizers, or just utilize the existing refrigerator compartments. Regardless, a couple minutes spent organizing this appliance is well spent.

Get started:

1 Group like items together. Keep your dairy items on one shelf, condiments in the door, beverages together, cheeses together, produce in produce drawers, etc.

2 Store your taller bottles and containers in the back and shorter in the front.

QUICK TIP: Running short on storage? Use clear, stackable containers to group like items together that don't fit in the drawers.

QUICK TIP: Keep produce freshest by keeping vegetables and strawberries at the high-humidity setting and most fruit at low humidity in the crisper drawers.

How to Organize Spices

How much you cook and bake will determine what your spice storage will look like, but a few simple steps can help with sorting and locating those spices and herbs.

Get started:
1 Sort spices by purpose (baking or cooking) and keep them separate. Take it one step further by separating by type (herbs, spices, blends, seasonings, etc.).
2 Alphabetize herbs and spices to make it easier to find what you need.
3 If you don't know when you purchased the spices or you open the jar and can't smell the spice, it's probably time to give it a toss. Most spices have a 6-month-to-1-year life span.
4 Add an organizational tool like a turntable, a spice organizer, or a tiered shelf.
5 Put everything back in a way that

makes sense for your storage space and cooking and baking needs.

 QUICK TIP: Small canning jars make a great storage solution for storing spices. Purchase spices in bulk and decant them into jars for a more uniform look.

BATHROOMS

BATHROOM SPEED CLEANING CHECKLIST	
Use this checklist for your weekly bathroom cleaning routine or for when you need to get this job done quickly.	
Counters and sinks — Clear off your counters and sinks	
Mirrors — Spray and wipe clean. I recommend a glass and mirror microfiber cloth for lint- and streak-free mirrors. Keep this cloth handy and reuse in each bathroom.	
Sink, toilet, and bathtub or shower — Quickly spray with your disinfecting cleaner. If you don't use a tub or shower regularly, you don't need to clean it weekly.	

Toilet — Do a quick clean with your preferred toilet cleaner and brush.	
Repeat these steps in each bathroom. Once you've done that, go back to the first bathroom and complete these steps:	
Sink, toilet, and bathtub or shower — Wipe off the cleaner using a separate cloth or paper towel for each to avoid cross contamination. Don't forget to clean the base of your toilets too!	
Place dirty cloths in a container and discard the paper towels.	
Repeat these steps in each bathroom.	

How to Organize Toiletries

Curb the counter clutter! All the lotions and potions in a bathroom can quickly take over and create quite a jumbled mess. If you want to set up a little more organization in your bathroom and you want to compartmentalize things a bit, organizing toiletries is a great place to start.

Gather your supplies:
- garbage bag
- all-purpose spray cleaner

- microfiber cloth
- containers to store toiletries in

Get started:
1 Start by removing everything from the space.
2 Spray the surfaces with all-purpose cleaner and wipe clean.
3 Sort/toss/recycle every single item in the cabinets or drawers.
4 Determine how many bins or containers you'll need for your categories and the space you have. Here are a couple categories to get you started:
    - teeth and mouth
    - sun and travel
    - ear, nose, and throat
    - manicure and pedicure
    - first aid
    - kids' remedies
    - pain relievers
    - tummy trouble
5 Place the items that you are keeping in their correct bin and return the bins to the space.

QUICK TIP: Make preliminary labels on a sticky note and then once you've determined final categories, go ahead and label everything.

BEDROOMS

Three Daily Tasks for a Tidy Bedroom

Once you have a clean bedroom, there are three basic daily tasks that you should put into place to keep it tidy. Added up, these tasks should take about 2–3 minutes to complete every day.

1 Make the bed every morning. This simple task will keep your bedroom looking neat and clean and it will also keep the bed clear of clutter.
2 Declutter surfaces daily — keep stacks of books, papers, and other miscellaneous items off nightstands and dressers.
3 Put clean and dirty clothing where it belongs — hanging up, in a drawer, or in a hamper.

How to Quickly Clean a Bedroom

Having an easy method for cleaning a bed-room is a great way to keep your bedroom clean all the time. Follow these simple steps and you'll find that your bedroom is not only easier to clean but it stays that way for longer.

Gather your supplies:
- dusting cloth or duster
- basket for items to relocate
- garbage bag for things to toss
- vacuum cleaner

Get started:
1 Set a timer for the amount of time you want to spend doing a quick cleaning of the bedroom.
2 Gather any items off the floor and flat surfaces. Place them in a laundry hamper, the garbage, or in the basket for items to relocate.
3 Do a quick dusting of the surfaces in the bedroom. Move quickly, concentrating on dusting furniture.
4 Vacuum the floor.
5 Make the bed and fluff the pillows.
6 Return anything that needs to be relocated.
7 Catch up on any unfolded clothes if

you still have time.

If you want to do a bedroom deep clean, go back to Week 4 of the 28-Day Simply Clean Challenge (page 115) to clean your bedroom from top to bottom.

How to Organize a Nightstand

An organized nightstand is not only a nice finishing touch in a bedroom, but it's also an integral part of creating a sense of calm and relaxation.

Get started:

1 Remove everything and wipe the nightstand clean.
2 Keep just the necessities on your nightstand:
   - a book or two
   - put hand lotion, lip balm, etc., in a cute container to corral these items and to keep them tidy
   - if your nightstand has a drawer, consider using a drawer organizer to keep things neat
   - a lamp

How to Organize Socks and Undies

The easiest way to start this process is to empty the space where you keep socks and undies. If you need some type of drawer organizer to keep your drawer a little neater, now's the time to add that to the list. I use small plastic shoeboxes in drawers to keep the socks and undies sorted.

Get started:
1 Completely empty the space or drawer and wipe it clean.
2 Toss any socks or undies that have holes, don't fit, don't have matches, or you just don't like anymore. If there's an item that you haven't worn in 6 months to a year, get rid of it.
3 Group like items.
4 Return the keep items back to your drawer or space. Fold neatly or toss in a box or small bin.

LIVING SPACES

Living rooms, one-room apartments, family rooms, dens, and basements can all fall under the category of living spaces. Every home has its own unique layout and circumstances, but one thing is certain: living spaces are typically the hub of the home. With some care and upkeep the living spaces can function as inviting and welcoming places that make sense and stay clean and organized most of the time.

Tips for a Clean and Organized Entryway

Keep your entryway in tip-top shape with a good cleaning and a few organizational tools. First, clean it up!

Gather your supplies:
- broom and dustpan
- vacuum cleaner
- microfiber cloths
- window cleaner
- dish soap and warm water

Get started:
1 Sweep outside the entry area first and shake out any rugs.
2 Vacuum the rug or carpet at the door.
3 Wipe down the front door with warm water.
4 Clean windows.
5 Vacuum and wash the floor, and tidy up your coat closet if you have one.

Once your entryway is clean, add storage. Stick to the basics and make sure you have a place to hang coats. Add hangers and a coat rack if necessary. Contain items with baskets and bins. If you frequently entertain, leave slippers and socks for guests to slip on — this also serves as a nice hint to your guests that they should remove their shoes (without your asking) and makes them feel right at home at the same time.

QUICK TIP: Put together a kit for clothing and shoe care and keep it in your entryway closet. Use a lidded box or basket and keep a couple items that work for your family and any guest mishaps. A lint roller, sweater shaver, stain pretreater, shoe polish, and any other items that you might use and need are perfect little items that you can add to a kit.

How to Decorate So Dusting Is Easy

If you keep your decorating simple, dusting and cleaning up can also be simple. I am by no means a minimalist, but I do find that keeping these unwritten rules in place when decorating can be helpful: Keep it simple. If you love it, keep it out. If you don't love it and it isn't useful, get rid of it. Look around your space; if there are things on display that you don't know why you have out, do yourself a favor and lose them.

Decorating is personal. It reflects your style, your memories, your life. Decorate with things that reflect you and your family. You won't mind cleaning around them if you love them. Follow these guidelines in your decorating to make cleaning easy.

1 **Keep surfaces clear.** Clear surfaces are always easier to clean than full surfaces.

2 **Be ruthless about getting rid of stuff.** If you are holding on to things that you no longer *need, want,* or *love,* it's time to get rid of them. Decorate with what you love. If you don't love it, don't keep it around.

3 **Declutter often.** Clutter can be a big problem. Deal with it daily to keep it away.

4 **Do a clean sweep.** Completely clear surfaces in a room, clean them, and let them breathe for a bit. If you're unsure of what to decorate a surface with, remove everything and add back little by little until you reach a look that you love.

5 **Utilize smart storage.** When you buy furniture, look for pieces that serve multiple purposes. Coffee tables with small doors can store games and puzzles. A dining room buffet can hold dishes, linens, and other dining room items.

Once you have clean and clear surfaces, a weekly once-over with a dusting wand can realistically take 15 minutes. Pick up larger items and dust under them, put them back, and keep going. If you find that dusting takes you longer than 15 minutes, you might want to set a timer to keep you on task — divide it up by floors or rooms to make it a little more manageable. Remember that every week that you continue to dust routinely, dusting gets easier and easier.

Toys in Living Spaces

If you have kids, and feel like your home looks like a toy store, you probably need to reevaluate your toy situation. Figuring out a system for containing the toys is crucial to keeping things simple and easy to put away. Regardless of the size of your family room, you can follow these simple steps and ideas and figure out a system for storing toys in this much-used area of your home.

I have a couple rules for toys in main living spaces, and they seem to keep toys from taking over while still allowing for creative play and lots of fun. With three kids with different interests and at very different ages, most of the toys in our family room are toys that my youngest plays with because he isn't in school all day yet and doesn't get to play in his room unsupervised like the older two. Teeny-tiny toys stay in containers in the oldest kids' bedrooms so they aren't a choking hazard to the littlest one.

This system works well, and hopefully it'll give you some ideas for organizing and including toys in your living space without feeling like a toy store threw up all over your house. I have four main considerations that I use for storing and keeping toys: contain, separate, hide from view, and adjust as necessary.

1 **Contain.** I love using baskets to store toys — I like the soft look they give, and as a bonus, they conceal what's inside. When everything's picked up and put away the room as a whole has a neat and tidy appearance. I always look for baskets with handles to give them some portability as well.

2 **Separate.** Separating toys into baskets or containers also makes it easy to take out one or two things at a time, which in turn makes it easier to pick up and put away. The basket can also be taken to another room or area of the house and easily picked up and put away.

3 **Hide from view.** I don't know about you, but clutter makes me crabby. Toys

strewn from one corner of the house to the next is fine while they're being played with, but when that time is over I want them to be put away quickly and easily. We use a bookcase and baskets to house most of the toys and some toys are hidden in our television console. Use the storage that you have and get creative with how you store toys — keep it simple and easy.

4 **Adjust as necessary.** As kids grow and their interests change, take a look at what's out and what can be passed down and donated. Make sorting through toys and playthings a normal occurrence in your home. It also teaches kids that you don't need as much stuff as you think you do. It's amazing to me how few toys they actually play with on a daily and weekly basis — it seems like it's the same one to three things over and over. Sometimes you have to assess and reassess the situation to determine what works for a specific stage or age or individual child.

CLOSETS

Closets can feel like a blessing and a curse. They're great if you have them, but they can also pose a whole new set of problems. Keep your closets clean and organized and you'll save time every single day by not having to search for that shirt or step over a pile of laundry.

The Best Way to Clean and Declutter Any Closet

A cluttered closet can give you an over-whelmed feeling. It's hard to locate what you need quickly and it can be a time suck. By cleaning and decluttering a closet correctly the first time, you'll find that just returning things where they belong right away is really all the maintenance that this space requires.

Gather your supplies:
- garbage bag
- relocate basket
- vacuum cleaner
- microfiber cloth
- all-purpose spray

Depending on the space, make sure you have the time it takes to empty, sort, and reorganize the space. Use these four simple categories — toss, donate/sell, relocate, keep. Put everything you come across into one of these categories and keep moving until you've decluttered your closet.

Get started:
1 Remove everything.
2 Sort and purge completely.
3 Wipe the space clean.
4 Vacuum the floor.
5 Group like items together.
6 Return the items back into your closet.

Organizing Your Closets for Efficiency

Closets can become a dumping ground, a black hole, or induce feelings of overwhelm. But keeping them organized doesn't have to be difficult. Simply put a couple systems into place and watch them run themselves. The closet rules below will keep your closets working for you, not against you.

1 **Go through closets and donate or toss outgrown and worn-out clothing.** Once you've purged clothing that is obviously not worth holding on to, determine what you haven't worn in 6 months and donate or toss those items.
2 **Not sure if you should keep something?** Turn the hanger around — if you or a family member doesn't wear the clothing in a month or two, find a new home for it.
3 **Group clothing with like items** — clothing is easier to find when it's

grouped with like articles. Group long-sleeved shirts together, short-sleeved shirts together, pants together, etc. With everything in its proper spot every time, you'll always be able to locate that favorite article of clothing in minutes.

4 **Create a hand-me-down bin.** If you have younger children or are saving clothes for other children, keep a bin in the closet pre-labeled with their current size and ready to be put into storage. When your child outgrows outfits, put them in the bin, and when the bin is filled up bring it to its storage spot. This is also a great solution if you're dieting or going through maternity clothing.

 QUICK TIP: Keep a small donate basket or bin in each family member's closet — when it's filled up, bring the contents to your favorite donation spot or pass on to a friend or family member.

LAUNDRY ROOM

I don't love doing laundry, but I can honestly say that I enjoy it now more than I ever have. This is a bold statement considering how much laundry our family of five produces. Here are four ways I have found to make laundry easier:

Four Things That Make Laundry Easier

1 Find a laundry soap or detergent that you love and that works consistently well. Whether it's the smell that you love, the ease of use, or the packaging, whatever it is that trips your trigger, use it and love it.

2 Keep the products simple. One or two products is all you really need in the laundry room or area — keep it clean and uncluttered.

3 Use the same color of towels and sheets. This allows them to be washed together and keeps washing them a breeze. I prefer white towels and white sheets — they can be washed on hot, which keeps them looking bright white and fresh for longer.

4 Involve the family. Teach even the littlest ones how to fold and put away their own laundry. I don't strive for perfection on this one, I just look for helpers, and that makes all the difference.

Laundry Every Day, or Laundry Day?

If you have piles and mountains of laundry that are seemingly insurmountable, you need to figure out a system that works. I am a firm believer in doing at least one load of laundry every day, but I also know that that method doesn't work for every person and every situation. I think that having a couple strategies in place is more helpful than the method itself. Choose one method and commit to making it work. If you're undecided, try doing one load of laundry daily — it'll change your laundry life.

Laundry Every Day

I developed this method for myself because I'm easily overwhelmed with full laundry baskets. Like, overwhelmed to the point of full denial and avoidance. If full laundry baskets don't make you feel anxious, then you're probably more of a laundry day person. The key to making the laundry every day process work is to take one load of laundry from dirty to folded and put away every day.

1 First figure out a simple laundry schedule of what gets washed on each day of the week. Or have one basket that everyone puts their dirty clothes in and

wash that at the end of each day.

2   Short on time? Put a load of clothes in at night and set your machine (if you have the option) to run at 4 or 5 a.m. Put those clothes in the dryer right away when you get up and fold before you leave in the morning or in the evening before bed.

Laundry Day

If you'd rather have all your laundry done and every laundry basket emptied out on the same day, this is the method for you. Here's the most efficient way to tackle laundry day:

1   Gather all the laundry in the house and put the baskets or hampers within reach of the laundry room. Line them up in order of what's going in the washing machine first to last. My recommendation is to start with adult clothes — do one load of whites and one load of darks per adult. You could also combine these clothes into two loads instead of four. Next in line is the kids' laundry (one basket per child — no sorting, all of it goes in the same load on cold). After all the clothing has been washed, it's time for sheets, towels, and finally cleaning rags.

2 While each load is washing and drying, fold, hang, and put away each and every load as soon as it comes out of the dryer. Depending on wash and drying time, this will most likely go on all day long, but it just takes minutes to fold and put away the clothing in between each load.

3 Once the laundry is done, run a cleaning cycle on the washing machine and leave the door open and walk away from the laundry room until next week.

Is there an in-between? Absolutely! Maybe you want to do laundry every other day or every third day. How would that work? If that's you, you'll need to have a laundry schedule much like the daily laundry schedule, where specific things are washed on specific days — kids' clothes on Mondays, adult clothes on Thursdays, and sheets and towels on Saturdays. The key to a laundry compromise is that you have to be consistent to make it work. If your schedule is ever-changing and you don't know if most Mondays you can wash a few loads of clothes, try one of the more extreme laundry methods — laundry day or laundry every day.

CHAPTER EIGHT:
HOW TO CLEAN ANYTHING

Ever wonder how to clean a showerhead or a matttress or leather furniture? I've got you covered. Cleaning shouldn't be complicated, but some areas and items complicate things. Use this as your resource for cleaning quickly and efficiently.

KITCHEN

How to Clean and Maintain Small Appliances

Small appliances make the kitchen go round but they also present a couple issues — where do you store them and how do you clean them? My rule of thumb for storage of any small appliance is that if it's not used at least two times a week, it gets stowed away. On our counters I keep the coffeepot, coffee grinder, and toaster. Can you tell what my priorities are? Determine what to store away and you'll free up a little counter space. Once you've figured out what can stay and what can go, having a simple and effective way to maintain any small appliance and keep it clean is key.

How to Clean the Surfaces of Small Appliances

If you have a crusty blender or flour from Christmas cookies on your mixer, you probably need to start getting in the habit of giving them a quick wipe after each use. I use the same cleaner that I use to clean counters (marble and granite cleaner — see page 306) on small appliances. It does a great job of cleaning and it will kill germs as well. Spray liberally, let sit for a couple minutes, and wipe clean with a microfiber cloth. Put the small appliance away and wipe the counter, too.

How to Clean a Drip Coffeemaker

If your coffeemaker is running slow or you can't remember when you cleaned it last, you might need to give it a little cleaning. This isn't the most pleasant-smelling process, but you'll love the results.

Gather your supplies:
- white vinegar
- cold water
- microfiber cloth

Get started:
1 Rinse out the carafe, basket holder, and reusable filter (if you have one).
2 Fill the carafe half full with white distilled vinegar and then fill to the top with cold water.
3 Pour the vinegar and water mixture into the water reservoir and begin brewing. Halfway through, turn off your coffeemaker and let it sit for 30–45 minutes. This allows the vinegar solution to settle in the inner workings of your coffeemaker and remove those hard-water deposits that can slow your machine down.
4 After 30–45 minutes, finish up the brewing cycle. Pour out what's in your coffeemaker and refill the water chamber with fresh, clean water.
5 Run clean water through your coffeemaker at least three times, or until the water is clear and the vinegar smell is gone.
6 Use a damp microfiber cloth with a dot of soap or a dab of white vinegar to wipe the exterior of the coffeemaker.

Wash the carafe and filter basket in hot, soapy water and allow it to dry.

How to Clean a Single-Serve Coffeemaker

There has been a lot of negative press recently about single-use coffeemakers and all the germs that have the potential to breed in their inner workings. A simple cleaning process will take care of that as well as remove those hard-water deposits that build up and make your coffeemaker brew slowly.

Gather your supplies:
- white vinegar
- cold water
- microfiber cloth

Get started:
1 Unplug and remove any removable pieces. This includes the water reservoir, K-Cup basket, and drip tray. These pieces can all be washed in warm, soapy water and left to drip dry.
2 Use a clean, damp microfiber cloth or paper towel to wipe the entire exterior of your machine. Give the K-Cup basket a little attention to get any coffee grounds that might be hanging on.
3 Reassemble the machine and plug it back in.

4 Fill the water reservoir half way with white distilled vinegar and then fill to the top with cold water.
5 Turn on the machine and run a cycle without inserting a K-Cup. Discard this solution and repeat this step until the water tank is empty.
6 Fill the tank with fresh, cold water and run through the cycle again without a K-cup. Dump the water and repeat until the vinegar smell is gone.

How to Clean a Toaster or Toaster Oven

The crumbs that can accumulate in a well-used and well-loved toaster or toaster oven can make the appliance work less efficiently and it just plain looks bad. Regular cleaning is the key to keeping your toaster or toaster oven running smoothly.

Gather your supplies:
- natural, plant-based dish soap
- warm water
- microfiber cloth

Get started:
1 Unplug the toaster or toaster oven. Remove the crumb tray and wash it with warm water and a squirt of dish soap.

Soak and scrub if necessary and dry thoroughly.

2 Turn the toaster or toaster oven upside down over the kitchen sink and shake out the toaster. Refrain from putting anything inside the toaster like a kitchen knife or on the heating elements, as that runs the risk of damaging them.

3 Wipe down the exterior of your small appliance and return it to its place on the counter.

How to Clean and Maintain Large Appliances

How to Clean a Dishwasher

Mineral deposits and food particles can build up in your dishwasher and prevent it from cleaning as well as it should. Add cleaning your dishwasher to your monthly or quarterly task rotation — your dishes will be cleaner and your dishwasher will run more efficiently.

Gather your supplies:
- white vinegar
- microfiber cloth
- small brush

Get started:

1 Start with a clean and empty dishwasher. Wipe the edges and the seal with white vinegar — the white vinegar will remove limescale and hard-water deposits.

2 Remove the bottom rack and check for any food particles or blockages. If your dishwasher has a filter, remove it and rinse under warm water.

3 Pour a cup of vinegar in the bottom of the dishwasher. Run the dishwasher on a quick wash, hot, sanitize cycle.

4 When the dishwasher has completed its cycle wipe dry with a microfiber cloth or allow to air-dry.

How to Load, Run, and Unload a Dishwasher

If you're a dish rinser, rinse the dishes — a dishwasher is designed to get all the food off the dishes, but a quick rinse ensures that the dishes won't need to be rewashed. If you don't rinse the dishes and you are happy with the performance of the dishwasher, by all means skip this step.

QUICK TIP: Use a small colander when rinsing silverware in the sink and to keep utensils contained after meals for easy dish washing or dishwasher loading. No knives down the disposal, and it makes it easy to put the silverware in the dishwasher — just bring the colander over and load the silverware into the dishwasher's cutlery basket.

Get started:

1 Stack dishes on the counter according to type if you aren't ready to load the dishwasher yet (i.e., you need to unload the dishwasher). This is a time-saver when it comes to loading the dishwasher because everything is all set to be placed in together.

2 Keep a standard format of glasses on top and plates and bowls on the bottom. Arranging the same glasses and plates together simplifies the putting away of the dishes — stack or group on the counter above the dishwasher and put them away.

3 Wash your sponges in the dishwasher nightly to keep them germ-free. Did

you know that the kitchen sponge is the dirtiest thing/place in most homes? Gross! If you have a sanitize cycle on your dishwasher, use this every time you run the dishwasher to kill germs on dishes, sponges, etc.

4 Make sure that the spray arms aren't blocked by a large pot or pan to ensure that the dishwasher is able to get everything clean. It's so annoying to open the dishwasher and realize that half of the dishes were cleaned and the other half weren't — take a second to double-check for blockages.

5 Run the hot water in your sink before running the dishwasher. This way the water is hot from the start and can rinse and clean your dishes effectively.

How to Clean Stove Burners and Grates

The best remedy for cleaning stove burners and grates is to wipe up spills and drips right away. But when that doesn't happen, a quick and easy solution for cleaning up burned-on food and grease is essential. Make sure your burners and grates can be removed and washed before attempting this solution.

QUICK TIP: If you're making a big meal or one that you anticipate being a little messy, keep a damp bar mop cloth on the counter near the stove to wipe up drips and splatters.

Gather your supplies:
- natural, plant-based dish soap
- warm water
- salt
- baking soda
- microfiber cloth
- small brush

Get started:
1 Fill sink with warm water and a squirt of dish soap. Place stove burners and grates in the soapy water to start soaking.
2 Mix up a quick paste of equal parts salt (table salt or kosher salt) and baking soda — start with about a tablespoon of each. Add a little water and rub the paste on the stove accessories to remove grease and baked-on food.
3 Repeat if necessary, rinse, dry, and put back on your stove.

How to Clean an Oven

Cleaning an oven can be an overwhelming task, but it doesn't have to involve conventional smelly and toxic oven cleaners. If your oven has a self-clean option, I recommend starting with that — it is a little smelly and it will tie up your oven for a few hours, but it does a great job with bringing the oven back to like-new status. Simply run the self-clean option and when the cycle has completed, let the oven cool and wipe clean with a damp sponge. If you don't have that option or you don't want to wait a few hours for a clean oven, try this natural approach.

Gather your supplies:
- 1/2 cup water
- enough baking soda to make a paste — about 1/4–1/2 cup
- 1 tablespoon natural, plant-based dish soap
- spray bottle with warm water

Get started:
1 Mix the ingredients to make a paste — it will expand and bubble up a bit as the baking soda combines with the soap and the water.
2 Using a sponge, spread the paste all over your oven to coat. Let the mixture

sit for at least 15–30 minutes.

3 Spritz with the warm water and use a clean sponge to wipe down. Repeat the rinsing with a sponge and warm water until the oven is completely clean and residue-free.

How to Clean Stainless Steel Appliances

Stainless steel appliances look beautiful when they're clean, but 95 percent of the time they show fingerprints, smudges, and smears, making them look dirty. Different brands use different grades and types of stainless steel, making it even harder to find a cleaner that works to keep them looking new.

The first thing you need is a clean, soft cloth to apply your preferred cleaner to the appliance. My preference is a microfiber cloth — it keeps the lint away and will buff to a great shine. Try out a few cleaners and brands until you have found one that works to your liking.

I have four suggested methods for cleaning stainless steel appliances:

1 **Water.** Use water applied to a microfiber cloth and wipe with the grain until you get a shine and remove any fingerprints and smudges.

2 **White vinegar.** Use white vinegar ap-

plied to a microfiber cloth and wipe with the grain until you get a shine and remove any fingerprints and smudges. The vinegar will cut any greasy spots — be careful to only use a small amount.

3 **Club soda.** Spray directly on stainless and wipe with the grain.

4 **Olive or baby oil.** If you're looking to polish your appliances, a little oil will do the trick. Buff in the direction of the grain until you no longer see any oil residue.

When applying cleaner you need to wipe your cloth in the direction of the grain of the stainless steel. This is because dirt can get trapped in the grain, and going against the grain can also damage or dull the surface. This method not only cleans better, but your stainless steel will appear much cleaner this way.

How to Clean a Refrigerator and Freezer

Save time by cleaning out your refrigerator and/or freezer when it's not full. Choose the day of or the day before a planned grocery shopping trip. If you get in the habit of doing a little menu planning and grocery shopping on a specific day of the week (I like Fridays), right before you leave for the store, wipe down the shelves in the refrigerator as you're assessing what groceries you need for the week ahead.

Gather your supplies:
- 1 teaspoon natural, plant-based dish soap or castile soap
- 4–6 cups warm water
- 1 teaspoon baking soda
- microfiber cloth
- small brush

Get started:
1. Begin by emptying out the entire refrigerator and/or freezer. If you're cleaning both on the same day, empty and clean them one at a time to make sure the food stays at appropriate temperatures.
2. Take a look at expiration dates and separate things that are past their prime or are virtually empty. Rinse and recycle containers that you can reuse and toss or compost everything else.
3. Once emptied, it's time to wash shelves and drawers.
4. Put any drawers into a sink of warm, soapy water. Rinse and dry thoroughly.
5. Mix up the soap, baking soda, and warm water. Dip microfiber cloth in the solution and wring out the micro-

fiber cloth. Wash shelves and drawers and repeat as needed. Dry if necessary.

 QUICK TIP: After you've done a big refrigerator and freezer cleanup, get in the habit of wiping down the shelves before you go grocery shopping. By adding this simple step, you'll find that a big cleaning of the refrigerator and freezer won't be necessary because you're maintaining this space weekly.

How to Clean a Microwave

If you just melted a stick of butter in the microwave and it exploded everywhere or the microwave hasn't been cleaned in a while, this method will do the trick to clean out the microwave effortlessly. Alternatively you can always spray a nontoxic all-purpose cleaner in the microwave, let it sit, and wipe clean.

Gather your supplies:
- natural, plant-based dish soap
- large microwave-safe bowl or 4-cup glass measuring cup
- 2–3 cups water

- 1 lemon
- sponge

Get started:

1 Remove the glass plate in your micro-wave and put it in your sink. Hand-wash the glass plate in the sink with a squirt of dish soap.

2 Pour the water into the microwave-safe bowl or measuring cup.

3 Cut the lemon in half and squeeze the juice into a bowl of water and put the lemon in the water as well.

4 Place the lemon juice and water in the microwave and run it until the water boils (3–5 minutes).

5 Leave the water in the microwave for 15 minutes or so to steam-clean your microwave.

6 Wipe clean with a damp sponge.

 QUICK TIP: If you need a little more cleaning power, spray a little 50/50 solution of vinegar with the lemon water on the interior of the microwave and wipe clean.

BATHROOMS

Ever since I was little and had to clean my bathroom as a weekly chore, I've loathed the job. Spraying ammonia and water on the floor and wiping it up with old shirts was pretty much the worst thing ever in my teen mind. Seriously, no one likes to clean a bathroom, right? The main goal when cleaning a bathroom should be germ and bacteria removal. Getting in and out in a hurry is just a bonus. As a mom with little boys I can attest that cleaning the bathrooms now is nowhere near as bad as it was when I was thirteen. I do use better tools, but still, not even close. Needless to say, I've come up with some easy and effective methods for the cleaning bathrooms.

How to Properly Clean a Toilet

What's your least favorite thing to clean in the whole house? I'm going to take a stab in the dark and say the toilet. I'm also going to say that part of the reason that everyone hates cleaning toilets is because they aren't cleaned properly the first time and then they get gross and you need a mask and gloves to go in there and clean it properly. If you do this simple routine weekly, I can't promise you that you'll enjoy cleaning the toilet, but at least it won't be quite as unpleasant a task.

Gather your supplies:
- all-purpose or disinfecting cleaner
- microfiber cloth or paper towels (or wipes if you're in a pinch)
- toilet bowl cleaner and toilet brush

Get started:
1 Spray the toilet thoroughly with your favorite bathroom cleaner. If you don't have a favorite, try the DIY disinfecting cleaner on page 304 or keep a bottle of hydrogen peroxide with a sprayer attached in your bathroom and use it to disinfect surfaces. When I say spray thoroughly, I don't just mean the seat — spray the top, the back, the handle, the seat, under the seat, the base, basically every single part of the toilet.
2 Squirt the toilet with your favorite toilet bowl cleaner or use a disposable toilet bowl cleaner (my personal preference).
3 Let the cleaners sit for a full 10 minutes to clean and disinfect the surfaces.
4 Start at the top of the toilet and wipe all parts down to the base. Finish by wiping the area at the bottom of the toilet where it meets the floor. Use a fresh cloth or paper towel for each toilet to avoid cross-contamination and do not use this cloth on any other surfaces.

5 Scrub the toilet bowl, flush, and rinse the brush in the toilet water. Let the wand rest under the toilet seat to drip-dry a bit if necessary.

 QUICK TIP: Use a pumice stone to remove those pesky toilet bowl rings. Toilet bowl rings are the result of hard water and mineral deposits that develop from standing water in the bowl. No amount of scrubbing, harsh chemical cleaners, or bleach will completely remove this buildup. Pumice is a natural volcanic rock that does a great job of removing surface stains in toilet bowls without scratching the surface. Look for a pumice stone with a handle so you don't need to stick your hand in the toilet bowl in order to get the job done. Simply rub the pumice around the interior of your toilet bowl where the ring is, repeat if necessary, rinse, and flush.

Soap Scum Removal

Any bathroom can accumulate soap scum — it's part showering and bathing products, part minerals in water, and part not cleaning it after each use (who has time for that?). In other words, if you shower and bathe, you probably deal with some degree of soap scum in your life. I find that squeegeeing shower doors after every use or after every other use definitely cuts back on the soap scum, but if you haven't been doing that you probably need a couple tips to get rid of it in the first place.

If you are dealing with a thin layer of soap scum, grab an erasing sponge, wet it, and scrub. Rinse and repeat. There are also long-handled scrubbers on the market that do a great job of scrubbing off soap scum.

Rust Removal

If you have rust or mineral stains on fixtures or in your bathroom sink, the fix is simple. Saturate paper towels or rags with white vinegar and drape over fixtures. Let it sit for 15 minutes and rub with the cloth to eliminate the rust. Rinse, and repeat if necessary.

Mold and Mildew Removal

Mold in a bathroom is common because of the near-constant moisture and steam. Make sure you have proper ventilation to prevent mold and mildew from forming. You may need to consider recaulking or regrouting your tub or shower when stains, mildew, or mold issues persist. A professional can help you eliminate and eradicate the mold properly. If you have a little bit of mold a great way to remove it is to spray straight hydrogen peroxide on the spot(s). Let it sit for up to an hour and rinse. You can also try using the same process with just straight white vinegar, no rinsing necessary. If the hydrogen peroxide and vinegar don't work, you can add a couple drops of tea tree oil (melaleuca) to the mixture — see the recipe on page 308.

 QUICK TIP: Place a clean spray nozzle right on top of a hydrogen peroxide bottle. Keep the hydrogen peroxide in the brown container it came in because it loses its effectiveness when it comes in contact with light. Hydrogen peroxide will bleach fabric so be careful where and how you spray the solution. Repeat if necessary.

Shower Cleaning and Maintenance

If you have a shower in a bathtub or a separate shower, you know that they are not the easiest thing to clean. Solid surface, glass, or tile, each surface poses a conundrum when it comes to cleaning. Do you spray the walls and scrub and rinse? Spray the whole thing and attempt to clean it without slipping and breaking a hip? Then you have the soap scum and potential mold that's par for the course. Maintenance is the best way to keep the scum and mold away. Get that shower clean and use a couple techniques to keep it that way.

Put together a little shower cleaning caddy or container that you keep in your shower or bathroom to use on a daily or weekly basis.

Gather your supplies:
- daily shower spray
- shower cleaning spray
- squeegee
- grout brush
- wide-handled scrub brush

Get started:

DAILY:

1 Use a daily shower spray (see page 307) to keep soap scum and mildew away and to make it easier to clean.
2 Use a squeegee at the end of your shower to remove excess water and to prevent water spots.

1 Spray all-purpose cleaner on walls, tiles, shower surround, faucets, showerhead (see next section, below), etc. Let sit for 10–15 minutes. Scrub clean and rinse thoroughly.
2 Keep a grout brush and a handled wide scrub brush handy to scrub surfaces as necessary.

MONTHLY:

1 Use a scrub (powder or paste) to deep clean your shower.
2 If you have a lot of soap scum, start with scrubbing the shower first to get it perfectly clean and then apply the daily and weekly routine. Use a handled scrub brush to effectively clean the grout and tiles.

How to Clean a Showerhead

If your showerhead isn't working as strongly as it has in the past, or if you're noticing mineral deposits, use white vinegar to get it clean.

Gather your supplies:
- 1 cup white vinegar
- sturdy plastic bag
- rubber band

Get started:

1 Pour the white vinegar into the bag, lift it up to the showerhead, and submerge the showerhead in the vinegar. Make sure that all of the spray holes are covered.

2 Secure the bag to the showerhead with the rubber band.

3 Keep the bag on the showerhead for at least 3 hours. After several hours or overnight, remove the bag.

4 Rinse thoroughly and wipe dry.

How to Clean a Whirlpool or Garden Tub

A whirlpool or garden tub is more difficult to clean than a standard bathtub because of its jets and not so frequent use. Clean your tub with this method at least quarterly or before each use.

Gather your supplies:

- 1/2 cup white vinegar (to disinfect)
- 3–4 tablespoons powdered dishwasher detergent (to remove soap residue)
- microfiber or soft cloth
- small scrub brush or toothbrush

Get started:

1 Fill the tub with hot water well above the jets.

2 Add the detergent and vinegar to the water. (If there is mold present when you are cleaning the tub you can use bleach instead of vinegar.)

3 Turn the jets on high and run for 15 minutes.

4 Empty the tub and fill it with cold water above the jet level.

5 Turn on the jets and run for an additional 15 minutes to remove any remaining residue.

6 Use a small scrub brush or toothbrush to reach into the jets. Rinse if necessary.

7 Use a microfiber cloth and wipe away any residue.

8 Wipe the handles with white vinegar to clean and polish.

BEDROOMS

I might be guilty of piling up laundry on the bed and not dusting bedrooms often enough. I find the bedrooms the hardest places to keep clean. This is really silly considering how little time we spend awake in our bedrooms. They should be spotless. Let's face it, the bedroom isn't cleaned as often as it should be. Considering how much time (even though it's spent sleeping) we spend in the bedroom, make it as clean and dust-free as possible. You'll sleep better and you'll go to bed feeling more relaxed knowing that you don't have to put the pile of laundry away that you just pushed off the bed to the floor.

 QUICK TIP: Have a lingering stinky spot? Put a drop or two of your favorite essential oil (lemon, lavender, and cedar are great for freshening a drawer) on a cotton ball or cotton pad and tuck in a musty dresser drawer, a stuffy closet, smelly shoes, gym bag, vacuum cleaner bag, or canister, etc.

How to Wash Pillows

If you have never washed your pillows, don't be afraid to — they clean up beautifully. Down and synthetic pillows are fine for machine washing, but don't wash foam pillows, as they will disintegrate in the dryer. If your foam pillow has a protective pillow top type of cover, remove and wash that instead.

You'll need:
- washer and dryer
- gentle detergent

Get started:

1 Remove the pillowcase and pillow protector. If you don't use pillow protectors, go and get one for all the pillows at your house. Not only do they protect them, the pillows can go longer between cleanings.

2 Set your washer on a gentle, large cycle with warm water.

3 Wash at least two pillows at a time to balance the machine and no more than three pillows at a time to guarantee a thorough cleaning.

4 After your washer has completed its cycle, run it through the rinse cycle again. This is to make sure that all the detergent is removed from the pillow.

5 Run the spin cycle twice to remove any excess water and help the pillows dry more quickly.

6 Once your pillows are washed and the excess water has been wrung out, toss them in your dryer.

7 Dry on low heat. Stop the dryer every 30 minutes or so and rotate the pillows around to make sure that they dry thoroughly and evenly. You might need to repeat the drying cycle to make sure that the pillows are thoroughly dry.

How to Clean and Freshen a Mattress

Proper mattress care will keep your investment and your sleep in check. Make sure that you rotate your mattress quarterly, or at least every six months, to keep the distribution consistent throughout the mattress.

First things first: make sure that you are taking care of your mattress daily — use a waterproof mattress pad. A mattress pad will keep any potential stains off your mattress and keep your mattress clean longer. Just launder it regularly with your sheets. I toss the mattress pad in every other washing.

When you rotate your mattress, take a couple minutes to vacuum the top of it to remove any dust and dust mites. Make sure that the nozzle of your vacuum cleaner is clean and slowly vacuum all of the crevices and the surface to eliminate any dust mites and dust. It sounds gross, but this is a necessary step in cleaning your mattress. If you use a waterproof, sealed mattress pad this is a quick and easy step.

If you get a stain on your mattress, blot up as much as you can with a dry towel. Once you've removed as much as you can, use warm water on a clean towel and a little dish soap or laundry detergent to clean the surface stain. Repeat and blot until the stain has been lifted. If the stain isn't removed easily, use the upholstery attachment on a carpet cleaner to clean the area. Blot up any extra water with a clean towel and place a fan near the mattress to dry it more quickly.

 QUICK TIP: If your mattress needs a little freshening up, sprinkle about 1/4 cup of baking soda that has been mixed with 3–5 drops of your favorite essential oil all over the surface of your mattress. Let this mixture sit for about 30 minutes and vacuum it up with a clean hose attachment or nozzle on your vacuum cleaner.

LIVING SPACES

How to Clean Throw Pillows and Blankets

There's no reason to be stuck with dingy throw pillows and blankets when it's so easy to launder them at home. Of course, always check the tag on your throw pillows before washing.

Get started:

1 If a throw pillow has a cover, remove it and launder the cover separately from

the pillow. Chances are the cover is the only thing that needs to be laundered, so wash that and keep the insert out of the washing machine.

2 Wash pillow covers inside out on cold and gentle if needed.

3 If the pillow insert cannot be laundered, it can be tossed in the dryer on high heat with some clean tennis balls to fluff it up. The heat from the dryer will help to remove dust and eliminate germs and smells.

4 Dry pillowcases in the dryer on low or no heat to ensure no shrinking, or preferably line-dry.

5 Wash any throw blankets with throw pillows as long as they are the same color — lights with lights and darks with darks.

How to Clean Baseboards, Doors, and Trim

Cleaning baseboards, doors, and trim are tasks that sound daunting and overwhelming, but staying on top of the dirt and dust that accumulate is key to keeping these neglected accessories clean. I use four methods with success in our home — choose one that works for your home and situation.

1 Baby wipes make a great baseboard cleaner. You can use them on painted and natural wood because of their gentleness. They are safe for kids to use as well. If you have little ones that like to clean along with you, give them some baby wipes and send them in the direction of the trim. You can thank me later.

2 A simple mixture of warm water and a squirt of castile or gentle dish soap applied with a microfiber cloth is my preferred method for washing baseboards. As long as your cloth is barely damp, this is also safe for unpainted woodwork. I find that microfiber cloths are the best for this task because they do a great job at getting in the nooks and crannies of trim, but you can also use a sponge. Wring out your cloth or sponge frequently to remove excess water and wipe baseboards and/or doors to clean. No rinsing required!

3 If you are trying to remove stubborn scuffs and marks on white trim, use white foam erasing sponges.

4 If you are cleaning and polishing stained wood trim, treat it like furniture. If you're looking for a homemade cleaner and polish, mix up this simple

concoction and use it to clean all the wood work in your home:

- 3 tablespoons white vinegar
- 1–2 tablespoons liquid coconut oil
- 10 drops lemon essential oil

Put a couple drops on a soft cloth and work in the direction of the grain. Repeat throughout your home and buff if necessary.

How to Clean Furniture

Regardless of the rules you have in your home surrounding your furniture, it doesn't take long for food, fingerprints, dirt, and pet stains to make their way on the surfaces. Follow these simple steps for a basic cleaning of any type of furniture.

Gather your supplies:
- vacuum cleaner
- lint roller

Get started:
1 Remove all cushions and pillows.
2 Use the crevice tool on your vacuum cleaner to clean the space under cushions and in the cracks and seams. If you don't have a crevice tool, use a lint roller for similar results.
3 Finish with the upholstery tool attach-

ment. Before you get started, make sure that it is clean. Run this attachment over cushions, arms, backs, and sides of furniture.

 QUICK TIP: If you have pets, keep a lint roller handy. A quick roll over the furniture will keep the pet hair, oils, and dander from building up over time. If you have kids, this is a great job to hand over to them.

If you're unsure of the material that your furniture is made of or its cleanability, check with the manufacturer before cleaning it.

Upholstery Fabric

Check on the tags or with your manufacturer to see if you can wash the slipcovers of your upholstered furniture. It's amazing what a good washing will do to clean up your upholstered furniture. Wash as directed or on cold with a gentle detergent. Dry it partially in your dryer on low heat or air-dry. Put it back on your furniture while it's still slightly damp to get a good stretch and to eliminate wrinkling.

For little drips or spills, mix up this solution to safely clean it up:

Gather your supplies:
- 2 teaspoons dish or castile soap
- 1/4 cup warm water

Get started:
1 Mix the warm water and soap in a small cup or container.
2 Using the soft cloth, dip it into the mixture and dab it onto those stains.
3 Once the stains are gone, blot with a clean, dry cloth to absorb any liquid that remains.

Add a little water to remove any residual soap. You can also use a cotton swab for itty-bitty spots.

Leather

Leather is really good at hiding dirt and grime — the darker it is, the better it hides the dirt. Even though it may not look dirty, it probably is. Leather is durable and easy to clean. I use just two ingredients to clean up leather quickly.

Gather your supplies:
- 1 teaspoon castile soap
- 1 cup warm water
- microfiber or soft cloth

Get started:

1 Mix the soap and water in a bowl.
2 Using a clean microfiber cloth, dip a small amount of the soap mixture on the cloth and wipe onto the surface. Work in small sections and dry immediately.

Microfiber

Microfiber furniture is a popular option because it's durable and cleans up easily. Nevertheless, it still can be a bit of a dirt magnet and can easily show fingerprints and stains. Check to see if you can wash the slipcovers of your microfiber furniture before you spend the time cleaning the whole thing section by section. Washing them does wonders for bringing back that almost new look and feel.

If you can't clean the slipcovers in your washing machine, try it by hand. Here's how.

Gather your supplies:

• rubbing alcohol in a spray bottle — you can just put a spray top on the alcohol bottle or decant about 6 ounces into a spray bottle
• light-colored sponge with a scrubbing surface
• bristled cleaning brush with white bristles so there isn't any color transfer

Get started:

1 Work in small sections and spray the rubbing alcohol on the surface of the furniture.

2 Use the textured side of the sponge and scrub the surface gently but with a little pressure.

3 Repeat this over the entire surface, concentrating especially on the arms, sides, and backs where dust and dirt accumulate.

4 Let the furniture dry completely.

5 The final step is to fluff up the fibers. Use the scrubbing brush and scrub in a circular pattern until no brush strokes remain. Continue until the whole piece is fluffed.

How to Vacuum Effectively (So You Only Have to Vacuum Weekly)

Invest in the best vacuum cleaner that you can afford when it's time to buy a new one. I've learned that the hard way — no one wants to be going through vacuum cleaners every year. Clean it often and you'll have it around for a long time. If you feel like your vacuum cleaner needs a name because it's out in the house more than you'd like to admit, try using a couple deep cleaning tricks to make your vacuuming last a little longer. Sweep or vacuum up little messes daily as you see them or after meals and pull out the big appliance on Wednesdays for vacuuming day. You'll find that not only do your floors look better for longer but you're saving time all week long.

Gather your supplies:
- vacuum cleaner with attachments

Get started:
1 Use the crevice attachment to vacuum the edges in each room before you vacuum the carpet. If this takes too much time, or just feels too tedious, get this tool out only when you notice dirt as you're vacuuming.
2 Start each room in the farthest corner away from the door and vacuum your way out of the room.
3 Vacuum horizontally in each room.
4 Vacuum vertically in each room. You didn't read that incorrectly, you are going over the carpet twice. This technique is the best way to make sure that the carpet is lifted and the embedded dirt, pet dander, and pet hair is removed.

QUICK TIP: You can put a drop or two of your favorite essential oil on a cotton ball and put it in your vacuum canister or vacuum cleaner bag to freshen the air while your vacuum is running.

Two Ways to Wash Windows

Washing windows is one of those tasks that can be time consuming and frustrating, but it is something that you can tackle for yourself. If you want to quickly wash a window or two, you'll just need to mix up a little window and mirror cleaner (see page 304), spray, and wipe. Vinegar and rubbing alcohol combine to create a quick-drying and effective window cleaner. Spray, wipe with a microfiber cloth (in one direction) and left to right and top to bottom, and walk away. So easy.

When I'm washing a houseful of windows, I like to mix up a batch of heavy-duty window solution, grab my squeegee, and get started.

Gather your supplies:
- 4 tablespoons castile soap or a natural, vegetable-based dish soap
- 4 tablespoons of rubbing alcohol

- about 1/2 gallon of warm water in a large, flat container
- squeegee with a rubber blade and microfiber pad or sponge
- large bath towels for the floor
- microfiber cloths for drips

Get started:
1 Fill the container with the water and bring it over to your windows. Add soap and rubbing alcohol. Place the container on a large bath towel or two in case there are any drips or spills.
2 In order to wash windows this way, you need a squeegee. I like an extendable squeegee with a washable microfiber scrubbing pad.
3 Dip your squeegee in the solution, press the excess water out, and apply the pad to your window (do one window at a time).
4 Once you have scrubbed your window, work left to right and top to bottom with the rubber side of your squeegee. Wipe off any excess water on the squeegee as you're working. Use a microfiber cloth to wipe up any streaks and drips on your windows.
5 If your windows are dirty you'll see dirty water drips on the windowsills.

Tackle two cleaning tasks at the same time and take a minute to wipe up each windowsill as you go.

How to Clean Your Washing Machine Naturally

All washing machines need to be cleaned, which is an oxymoron if you really think about it. Why would you need to clean something whose job is to clean? This simple task can be done weekly or at least once a month. The result is a fresh and odorless washing machine that you know is clean. If you've ever had clothes or towels come out of the washer or dryer smelling musty or mildewy, you can most likely appreciate not having to rewash your wash.

You'll need:
- washing machine — if your washing machine has a self-clean option, you can omit the vinegar or non-chlorine bleach.
- enough white vinegar or non-chlorine bleach to fill your bleach dispenser — about 3/4 cup. Some washing machine manufacturers recommend only using chlorinated bleach. Follow the instructions for your specific machine or try this natural method.

Get started:

1 Add 3/4 cup white vinegar *or* non-chlorine bleach (not both) to the bleach dispenser or fill to its max level.

2 Look for the self-cleaning option on your washing machine — some washing machines have a separate cleaning cycle as an option. If you don't have that as an option, select the hottest water setting possible. Select the extra rinse option if your washer has that choice to make sure that the vinegar has been completely rinsed from the machine.

3 Allow the cycle to run until it has completed.

4 Once the washing machine has been washed, wipe out the bleach and fabric softener dispensers. These can be easily cleaned by simply removing and washing in warm, soapy water to remove any residue or by wiping them down with white vinegar on a cleaning cloth. Rinse and dry them thoroughly before reinserting them.

5 If you have a front loader, wipe down the rubber seal on the door, as it is a perfect hiding spot for mold and mildew. Pull back the rubber gasket and carefully wipe down the area with

white vinegar and a soft, white cleaning cloth. Rinse with a cloth dampened with water and dry thoroughly with a clean cloth to prevent any moisture buildup. If you have a top loader, wipe down the inside of the door and the seal.

6 After cleaning the inside of your washing machine, the door, and the seal, wipe down the exterior and control panel with an all-purpose cleaning spray to remove any dust and dirt buildup.

 QUICK TIP: Be sure to leave the door open to prevent moisture buildup in between loads and clean it inside and out every month. Leaving the door open will eliminate any mildew and smell in your washing machine.

How to Clean Your Dryer So It Works Efficiently

If you've ever opened your dryer expecting to find dry clothes only to open it up and find still-damp clothes instead, you probably need to give it a little cleaning. If a little cleaning doesn't do the trick, call a professional to check out the situation.

Gather your supplies:
- all-purpose cleaner
- microfiber cloth
- dryer vent cleaner
- vacuum cleaner

Get started:
1 Start by giving your dryer a thorough exterior cleaning. Spray the entire exterior with your favorite all-purpose cleaner and wipe with a microfiber cloth (the microfiber cloth will trap any lint or dust, making it easier to clean).
2 Remove and clean the lint trap.
3 Use a long-handled dryer vent cleaner to get any trapped lint.
4 Use the crevice tool on your vacuum cleaner to vacuum up any remaining lint.
5 Finish up by vacuuming under the dryer.

Stain Removal Chart

Stains are part of laundry life — knowing a few good tricks for getting out most stains will save your clothes. I'm always up for a challenge when it comes to laundry stains.

As an art teacher, I would send kids home with stain removal instructions pinned to their clothes. Parents loved it and I'm pretty sure it saved a shirt or two. I find that most of the time if I catch a stain right away and run it under cool water and blot it up, I can remove it. If that doesn't work I pretreat with a little laundry detergent or stain remover. If you wash something, check to see if the stain came out of the clothing and if it did, dry it. If it didn't, try to remove the stain again before drying it. If the unremoved stain goes through the dryer it will most likely set and be nearly impossible to be removed.

STAIN REMOVAL CHART
With a quick response, most stains can be removed. Here are some of my favorite ways to remove common stains. Once you've tried the method, launder as usual.
Bodily fluids — Blot and soak up with cold water and treat with oxygen bleach alternative.
Fruit and juice — Run under warm water and treat the stain with white vinegar. If the fabric is white, treat with hydrogen peroxide.

Grease and oil — Keep a piece of white chalkboard chalk in the laundry room and draw over any grease stains. If the grease or oil stain is larger, sprinkle a little cornstarch over the stain and a drop of dish soap.

Ink — Dab with a cotton swab dipped in rubbing alcohol.

Sweat — Mix up a baking soda and water paste and scrub with a clean toothbrush to dissolve perspiration. Soak in 1/4 cup oxygen bleach alternative and warm water in washing machine or a small laundry bucket for a couple hours or overnight.

Unknown stains — Rub with a bar of castile soap.

Wine — Blot with club soda or cool water and soak up stain.

CHAPTER NINE:
CLEANING THOSE
HARD-TO-CLEAN SPACES

Basements, garages, crawl spaces, attics —
those poor neglected spaces that would love
a little organization and rarely get it. We put
boxes and bins in their space for later and
never get back to it. Or is it just me? I still
have a few boxes from moving into our new
house eight years ago. Whatever your reason
for putting off cleaning and organizing these
spaces, don't let them get the best of you.
Give it your best shot and tackle the spaces
once and for all.

HOW TO SORT THROUGH BOXES
AND BINS THAT YOU HAVEN'T TOUCHED
IN MONTHS OR YEARS

If you have an unfinished basement or attic

space that feels more like a dumping ground for items you don't know what to do with or where to put, the best way to deal with this space is similar to organizing any other space but with a little more ruthlessness. The best part of organizing a basement or attic or going through these items is that you've already determined that you don't need those items on a daily basis. The worst part of organizing an attic or a basement is that you have already determined that for some reason you can't part with the items that you are still storing. Maybe you have boxes from your move that are unopened, or boxes from relatives, childhood, or other memories that you can't part ways with quite yet.

If you have boxes upon boxes upon boxes in a basement or attic, going through them in an afternoon is most likely not even close to realistic. My suggestion for dealing with the difficult-to-sort memorabilia from the past is to be thorough, with the goal of knowing exactly what is in each and every container that you intend to keep.

Gather your supplies:
- 3 boxes for sorting — label them donate/sell, relocate, keep
- garbage bag for items you're tossing
- timer

- index cards
- pen
- envelopes for the bins (or another labeling system)
- tape to attach the labels
- new boxes or bins if you need them (if the boxes are falling apart or not going to stand the test of time).

Get started:
1. Set up a station in your basement with a table or writing surface, a chair, your sorting boxes, and a garbage bag.
2. Start with one box or bin — set your timer for 5–10 minutes and completely sort through that box or bin in that amount of time. Every single item is going to go into one of the four categories — toss, donate/sell, relocate, keep. Don't worry about doing anything with those items yet, just keep working through your stuff. Once you've gone through that box or bin, set your timer again and move on to the next one. Keep the original boxes if they are worth keeping, but do not put anything back in them (yet).
3. Move on to another box and another box until you feel like you're making some progress. If you have five boxes to

go through, this can easily be done in an hour or so. If you have a basement full of boxes, this will take some time. Take a deep breath and keep going.

4 Once you have completed one section or all of your basement, it's time to figure out where everything is going to go. The toss bag goes in the garbage, and the donate/sell box goes in your car and to your favorite donation station (my preference because it's out of the house) or in a spot for resale. The relocate box is for things that need to move out of the basement and up into your home, and the keep box will need to be re-sorted for further storage.

5 Once you have enough items to make up a box or more, group these items in ways that make sense. Dishes from Grandma, high school memorabilia, baby clothes — put like items together and pack them away neatly. If there's something that you look at and aren't sure if you want to continue storing it, put it in the donate bin and be done with it.

6 Before you close the lid on that box or bin, take an index card and title the box. You can label them from A to Z or number them from 1 to whatever. The most important thing about your

system is that it makes sense to you and it works how your mind works. Once you've determined your system, you need to label your cards and boxes. Under the title put exactly what's in the box so there's never any question — like this:

Dishes from Grandma (box 1:2)
6 dinner plates
8 luncheon plates
6 teacups and saucers
gravy boat

Dishes from Grandma (box 2:2)
2 serving bowls
serving plate

Get as specific as you'd like — you can even take a picture of what's in the box and put it in the envelope with the inventory card or on the outside the box. I find that taking your organization and storage to this level really ensures that every single item that gets to take up space in the basement or attic is worth keeping.

How to Clean Icky Spaces in a Basement, Attic, or Garage

If you have a dreaded spot in your basement,

attic, or garage that haunts you with its cobwebs, dead insects, or something else that's just plain gross, I'm here to tell you that you can clean it up and, once you do, you'll feel much better about it. Truth be told, I typically enlist the help of my husband for those icky spaces, but I do know how to clean them up and even help on occasion.

Gather your supplies:
- vacuum cleaner (we keep a Shop-Vac for these icky areas in the basement)
- large broom
- garbage bag
- all-purpose cleaner
- cleaning cloths or paper towels
- mop and bucket (if floor or wall washing is needed)
- heavy-duty floor cleaner

Get started:
1 Depending on what you are trying to accomplish, divide your work into these specific zones.
2 Start with Zone 1 and work through to Zone 3.

Zone 1 — ceilings: Use a broom or your Shop-Vac to get rid of any cobwebs on the ceiling beams or rafters.

Zone 2 — walls and corners: Starting at where the ceiling meets the wall, dust down to the ground — use a large broom and/or vacuum to gather bugs, cobwebs, and dust. If you need to wash the walls, use your mop and bucket and follow the wall cleaning with a wall washing. Work from the back of the space and go from left to right, rinsing often and changing the water as soon as it looks dirty.

Zone 3 — floor: Starting at the farthest corner of the space, vacuum or sweep from left to right toward the door. Once the floor has been vacuumed or swept, grab your mop and bucket and heavy-duty floor cleaner and wash the floor in the same pattern — start at the back and move your way out the door.

Cleaning a garage or basement thoroughly is daunting, and it can be icky, but it can be done and done well with a plan and a couple heavy-duty tools.

CLEANING YOUR CAR AND KEEPING IT CLEAN

Regardless of how much time you spend in your car, you know how quickly it can go from clean to chaos. Let's start by cleaning it up and then putting a couple systems in place to keep it that way.

Gather your supplies:
- garbage bag
- lint roller
- Shop-Vac
- all-purpose spray cleaner
- window cleaner
- microfiber cloths

Get started:
1 Start by gathering up any trash that's accumulated.
2 Toss what can be tossed and bring inside any receipts or items that you need to keep.
3 Take your car to a quick car wash and vacuum it out there if you'd like or wash and vacuum at home.
4 Use your lint roller to grab any remaining lint, grass, and dirt.
5 Spray and wipe windows.
6 Wipe down and clean car seats.
7 Spray and wipe any cup holders and other plastic accessory pieces.
8 Dust and wipe the dashboard.

QUICK TIP: Put a couple systems in motion to keep your vehicle neat and clean. A messy car can induce stress in a possibly already stressed situation. Do what you can to keep things calm and easy.

Keep a small bucket or basket in the car for garbage.

If you're in your car often, keep a mini cleaning kit (lint roller, mini hand duster, baby wipes) together so you can clean up the car while you're stopped in traffic or in the carpool lane.

Stop eating in the car if you can, if you can't, make sure you're bringing *all* the garbage out of the car and throwing it away every time you have food in the car.

How to Clean and Organize Any Seldom Used Space

Have a space that you rarely use but need to clean or organize it? This space can be a garage, basement, attic, or crawl space. Or maybe you have a utility room that has so much stuff in it that it's become a fire hazard. We had a storage space in our first apartment that we stashed everything in — it was completely packed to the point that moving

285

anything was like a game of Jenga. Shelves or a storage system would have been a better option in that teeny tiny closet. Think through your space and figure out the best way to tackle it and get started. It's hard to make the time to organize these spaces, but it can be so worth it to have that overlooked space clean and organized once and for all. The plan for cleaning and organizing a seldom used space is similar to any other space.

Gather your supplies:
- vacuum cleaner (we keep a Shop-Vac for icky areas in the basement and garage)
- large broom
- garbage bag
- all-purpose cleaner
- cleaning cloths or paper towels

Get started:
1 Determine which spot you're going to work on — start small and make sure you can complete the task in a short time.
2 Set a timer for 10–15 minutes.
3 Completely empty the area to be organized and sort into four groups — toss, donate/sell, relocate, keep.
4 Sweep and/or vacuum if necessary.

5 Wipe down area with your favorite cleaner or wipes.
6 Return keep items to the formerly disorganized space and put the items away that you are relocating.

GETTING A HOUSE READY TO SELL AND HOW TO KEEP IT CLEAN FOR SHOWINGS

You're moving. Now what? Not sure where to start to get your house ready to go up for sale? And how in the world do you keep it clean and show-ready when you're still living in it? First things first: you need to pare your belongings down to the bare minimum — less stuff equals less mess. If you know you're going to put your house up for sale in the next few months, my recommendation is to go through the 7-Day Simply Clean Kick Start (Chapter 3) and 28-Day Simply Clean Challenge (Chapter 4). These challenges will get you in the habit of cleaning and tidying up every day, which in turn will be extremely helpful for getting the house show-ready at a moment's notice. If you don't have a month to devote to preparing the house, do the 7-Day Simply Clean Kick Start and then follow these steps to get it show-ready.

Get started:
1 Declutter the entire house — if you

287

don't want to move it, get rid of it.

2   Pack up any belongings you won't need for the next 3–6 months — put them in storage or bins out of sight.

3   Check light fixtures — make sure you have working bulbs in each and every light. Dust and clean lightbulbs if necessary.

4   Do a thorough dusting — ceilings, corners, vents, and surfaces.

5   Clear counters in the kitchen and bathroom — less stuff will make your home look larger and a less cluttered appearance sells houses.

6   Deep clean the bathroom — recaulk if necessary.

7   Deep clean the kitchen — clean cupboards and other areas that people will most likely peek into when looking at your house.

8   Clean all the appliances, inside and out.

9   Wash floors and baseboards.

10   Remove any personal items like pictures and items with your name on them.

11   Check the basement, attic, and garage for cobwebs and noticeable dirt and debris that could deter a future homebuyer.

12 Shampoo carpets — consider having this professionally done.
13 Wash windows inside and out — consider having this professionally done.

Now that your house is show-ready, you want to keep it that way! Make sure that you are doing your daily Simply Clean tasks (see page 47), and then once you have a showing, put these items on your list:

1 Wipe down kitchen counters.
2 Wipe fronts of appliances.
3 Put out fresh kitchen towels.
4 Quick sweep or vacuum where needed or in high-traffic areas.
5 Quick floor wash anywhere that might be needed.
6 Wipe down bathroom counters — keep cleaning wipes handy.
7 Clean toilets.
8 Put out fresh towels and rugs if necessary in the bathrooms.
9 Pick up toys and laundry.
10 Do a quick lint roll of any pet areas.
11 Hide dirty laundry — take it with you in your car if you need to.
12 Make sure beds are made.
13 Open window treatments so it's bright and airy.

14 Make it smell good — bake cookies (have some premade ones on hand), burn a candle, spritz something yummy — you want your future buyers to feel at home and to notice a homey smell, not the smell of pets, dirty laundry, or your most recent meal.

QUICK TIP: Put together a mini cleaning caddy for showings — keep cleaning wipes, floor wipes, a lint roller, a wand duster, a garbage bag, and any other items you find yourself needing to tidy up before showings. Grab the caddy, do a quick cleaning, and get out of the house.

HOUSE FOR SALE CHECKLIST

GET YOUR HOUSE READY TO SELL

- ❏ Declutter house
- ❏ Pack up unnecessary belongings
- ❏ Clean walls
- ❏ Clean light fixtures
- ❏ Check light fixtures
- ❏ Wash windows
- ❏ Wash baseboards
- ❏ Clean window treatments
- ❏ Clean mirrors
- ❏ Wipe switch plates
- ❏ Clean appliances — inside + out
- ❏ Deep clean kitchen
- ❏ Clean off counters (kitchen/bath)
- ❏ Deep clean bathrooms
- ❏ Remove personal items (pictures)
- ❏ Remove cobwebs — basement, garage, porch
- ❏ Check/fix caulk in bathrooms
- ❏ Clean carpets and floors
- ❏ _____
- ❏ _____
- ❏ _____
- ❏ _____
- ❏ _____
- ❏ _____
- ❏ _____

QUICK CLEAN CHECKLIST
FOR SHOWINGS

❏ Wipe down kitchen counters
❏ Wipe fronts of appliances
❏ Quick vacuum floors where needed
❏ Quick wash floors where needed
❏ Wipe down bathroom counters
❏ Clean toilets
❏ Put out clean towels
❏ Fluff pillows on sofas
❏ Make beds — arrange pillows
❏ Open window treatments
❏ Quick dust
❏ Burn a candle or use air freshener
❏ Take out all garbage
❏ Put out clean rugs
❏ Open window for fresh air
❏ Pick up toys and personal items
❏ Hide dirty laundry — take it with you if
   you need to!

❏ _____
❏ _____
❏ _____
❏ _____
❏ _____
❏ _____
❏ _____
❏ _____

■■■■

Part Six:
Cleaning Supplies
and Resources

■■■■

CHAPTER TEN:
SIMPLE CLEANING SUPPLIES
YOU CAN MAKE YOURSELF

Did you know that many of the ingredients in store-bought cleaning products are toxic? They can trigger allergies, asthma, headaches, and breathing issues, and some contain potential carcinogens. Why bring something toxic into your house? Cleaning with natural products and ingredients is safe and economical. I recommend one of three approaches — making your own cleaners, buying natural cleaning products without chemicals, or a combination of the two. Making your own cleaners is a lot less time consuming than you might think, and if you have the ingredients on hand you can whip up a batch of granite cleaner or window cleaner whenever you need it. No running to the store to stock up.

Start with making one or two simple cleaning solutions and I bet you'll be hooked. And the best part? By making sure everything you put on surfaces in your home is safe, you won't be doing any damage to the health of your family. This chapter will show you how to make organic cleaning products that are safe, cost just pennies per bottle, and smell so much better than the chemical-laden stuff!

THE FIVE MUST-HAVE INGREDIENTS

Let's say you are apprehensive and unsure of making your own cleaners. Having just a few ingredients on hand will allow you to mix up an effective and safe cleaner that you can use when you need it. Need to clean the oven or want to wash your windows and you just realized that you ran out of the blue stuff? Keep these five ingredients handy and you can clean a whole house.

1 **Water.** Water is the base for most cleaning solutions. If you want to keep your cleaners around for more than a week or two, use filtered or distilled water to make sure bacteria isn't lurking.

2 **White vinegar.** An acid, this natural

cleaning agent can be used for pickling and cooking, so you know it's safe to spritz around the house. One caution: because it's an acid, don't spray it on marble, granite, or other stone — the acid will etch away that pretty surface over time.

3 **Baking soda.** This baking ingredient packs a huge cleaning punch as a deodorizer, abrasive cleaner, and all-around base for cleaning pastes. Baking soda is the perfect odor absorber — sprinkle it in smelly garbage cans, on stinky carpet (let it sit and vacuum it up), and keep a box in your refrigerator or freezer to absorb odors.

4 **Castile soap or natural, vegetable-based dish soap.** Soap and water can effectively clean just about any surface. Have it handy to clean surfaces and to mix with other ingredients to make powerhouse cleaners.

5 **Hydrogen peroxide.** You know the stuff in the brown bottle? It's a natural disinfectant and when tested has been shown to kill germs more effectively than bleach. Keep it in the brown bottle — its disinfecting properties go away when exposed to light — and add a sprayer to make a disinfectant spray.

Spray on sinks, yucky cutting boards, counters, mildew, just about anywhere you want to knock out germs and bacteria. Let it sit for 5–10 minutes and wipe clean. (Hydrogen peroxide also lightens hair and fabrics so be careful where and how you spray it.)

Are you surprised that these are the must-have ingredients? I bet you already have three out of the five in your pantry or medicine cabinet. Gather them up and keep them in one place and you'll have the start of your own little DIY cleaning arsenal.

What if you already love making your own natural cleaners and want to up your game? Then you'll need these ingredients (you'll notice that my five must-haves are included):

- water
- white vinegar
- baking soda
- castile soap or natural, plant-based dish soap
- hydrogen peroxide
- washing soda
- essential oils (not necessary, but some good ones are tea tree, lemon, clove, peppermint, and lavender — see page

301 for my favorite cleaning combinations)
- kosher salt
- lemons
- rubbing alcohol and/or vodka
- bleach alternative powder

A Few Things You Need to Know About DIY Cleaners

1 Never, ever use vinegar on stone, granite, marble, etc.— vinegar's high acidity will etch away at your beautiful counters over time.

2 Homemade cleaners have a shorter shelf life because they don't have preservatives — though I mix up oodles of DIY cleaners and have never had one go bad. Mix up one batch at a time and you'll be fine.

3 The bulk of each cleaner is water — use filtered or distilled water to extend the shelf life of your cleaners, or boil and cool the water if you are unable to filter it. This keeps any microorganisms from tap water out of your cleaners.

4 All of the recipes that I provide are for 16-ounce spray bottles unless otherwise specified.

5 I recommend using glass spray bottles because they allow for the use of essen-

tial oils — essential oils can eat away at plastic over time.

6 Most recipes will require these supplies: measuring cup, measuring spoons, funnel (makes it easier to pour liquid ingredients into a spray bottle), spray bottle, labels (make sure you know what you mixed up!)

7 Once you've mixed your combination, simply close the spray bottle, shake, and *clean*!

Natural Versus Synthetic or Chemical Cleaners

If you're on the fence about natural versus synthetic or chemical cleaners, ask yourself when was the last time you felt a little lightheaded after cleaning the bathroom? Conventional cleaners aren't helping you — they're actually doing more harm than good to you and the environment. If you don't want to make your own cleaners (I don't make all of mine!), look for commercial cleaners that don't have warning labels like "Use in a well-ventilated area," "Wear gloves when using this cleaner," or "Contact poison control if you come into contact with this cleaner." Do your research and make sure that you keep cleaners away from children and pets. Look for formulas with natural ingredients that you recognize — there are so many options available! Some products that you are familiar with still include formaldehyde, artificial fragrances, and other toxic preservatives. My favorite resource is the Environmental Working Group at EWG.org — they rate cleaners from A–F, then list the potential harm.

If you're worried that you need to kill every germ in order to keep your family safe, that really isn't the case. I used to be that clean-everything-with-bleach person, but after researching and putting methods to use in my own home with three kids, I can assure you that you won't miss the promise to "kill 99.99 percent of germs." Interestingly, soap and water alone can remove most germs, and if you add a little vinegar or hydrogen peroxide to the mix you'll find that you're meeting that same almost 100 percent germ killing quota.

ESSENTIAL OIL COMBINATIONS PERFECT FOR CLEANING

You'll notice that I use a lot of essential oils. Essential oils are oils from plants — they are not fragrance oils. They can be pricey, but they are highly concentrated and last for what seems like forever. I add essential oils primarily for scent, but you'll also find that some have excellent germ-killing properties, making them a great solution for DIY cleaners.

Feel free to be a purist and buy one bottle of one essential oil and use that to scent everything. It'll be pure, fresh, and clean-smelling. But if you want to expand your scent palate, here are a couple fun combinations for your cleaners. Each recipe that lists essential oils has a drop count — add up your oil combination to make that amount. If a recipe calls for 10 drops of essential oils and you want to mix lemon and lavender, add 5 drops of lemon and 5 drops of lavender. Want a little more lavender and a little less lemon? Use 7 drops of lavender and 3 drops of lemon. Experiment to get your perfect scent combination. Most essential oil companies sell blends that work great as well. My absolute favorite combination and signature scent? Lemon and clove — it's warm, clean-smelling, and just yummy.

Citrus Scents — sweet, refreshing, energizing scents (use alone or combine)
- lemon
- orange
- grapefruit
- lime

Spicy Scents — warm, inviting scents (use alone or combine with a citrus scent)
- cinnamon
- vanilla
- clove
- ginger
- cardamom

Clean Scents — combinations that smell fresh and clean
- tea tree (also known as melaleuca)
- lemon + peppermint
- rosemary + peppermint + lavender
- pine + lemon + lime

Spa-like Combinations — if you need to be soothed while cleaning
- lavender + eucalyptus
- cedarwood + pine
- cardamom + peppermint + rosemary

Basic Cleaning Recipes — Five Recipes That You Need to Mix Up Now

All-purpose cleaner
This cleaner works perfectly on just about any surface you can dream up (except for marble, granite, and stone because of

the acidity/pH level). Even better, it's kid-friendly.

- 1 1/4 cups water
- 1/2 cup white vinegar
- 10 drops essential oils

Combine ingredients and pour into a glass spray bottle.

Disinfecting cleaner

- 1 1/4 cups water
- 1/4 cup white vinegar
- 1/4 cup vodka or rubbing alcohol (extra germ-killing properties in addition to the vinegar)
- 15 drops essential oils

Combine all ingredients and pour into a glass spray bottle. Spray surface and let sit 10 minutes before wiping.

Glass and mirror cleaner

Looking for clean and streak-free windows and mirrors? This quick-drying spray will do the trick! See my tips for how to wash windows on page 269.

- 1 1/2 cups water
- 1 1/2 tablespoons white vinegar

- 1 1/2 tablespoons rubbing alcohol
- 3 drops essential oils

Mix in spray bottle, spray liberally on surface or directly on microfiber cloth, and wipe.

Sink scrub

Cleaning the kitchen sink with this is part of my nightly kitchen cleaning routine. It works great and smells divine.

- 2 cups baking soda
- 20 drops essential oils (I recommend lemon + clove in this recipe, but feel free to substitute your favorites or eliminate altogether)
- container with a lid or a shaker top — a mason jar is a perfect container for this
- sink-safe scrub brush — I keep it under my sink in a vintage mason jar. Look for one with a removable head that you can toss in the dishwasher to sanitize as needed.
- castile soap or natural, plant-based dish soap (this is not added to the baking soda until it's used)

Pour baking soda into your container and add essential oils. Stir and combine with a kitchen knife. Wet sink and sprinkle liberally. Add a squirt or two of dish soap, scrub with a sink-safe scrubber or sponge, and rinse thoroughly.

 QUICK TIP: The sink scrub isn't just for sinks — sprinkle it anywhere you need a little abrasive cleaning action, add water, spray cleaner or soap, and scrub. Use it dry and sprinkle on mattresses and carpets as a freshener — let sit to absorb odors and vacuum it up.

Marble and granite cleaner
I am guessing that you can find more than just marble or granite to clean once you try this recipe — it's amazing! It's definitely one of my favorites!

- 3 tablespoons rubbing alcohol
- 1 1/2 cups water
- 1 teaspoon castile or dish soap (if you want your spray to smell like your dish soap, use that)

Mix and store in a glass spray bottle. I use this daily on the kitchen counters — it's perfect for granite.

SOME OTHER DIY
CLEANERS TO TRY

Once you've tried those five basics and you're ready to branch out a bit, or if you have a cleaning conundrum, there are so many more recipes that you can whip up to clean your house from top to bottom. Here are a couple more that are used the most often in our home.

Kitchen and Bathroom Cleaners
Daily shower spray
- 1/2 cup vodka *or* 1/2 cup white vinegar (if you have marble or granite in the shower use vodka)
- 1 cup water
- 10 drops essential oils

Mix and store in a spray bottle. Spray shower or tub daily after bathing. No rinsing required. This cleaner won't keep your shower or tub clean all the time but it will make it easier to clean and keep that soap scum at bay. Hooray!

Stainless steel cleaner
- White vinegar
- Microfiber cloth

Spray white vinegar directly on a microfiber cloth and wipe with the grain until you've buffed away any fingerprints and smudges. See page 243 for more tips and tricks on cleaning stainless steel.

Mold and mildew remover
- 1 cup water
- 1/2 cup hydrogen peroxide
- 20 drops tea tree (melaleuca) essential oil (tea tree oil is important in this recipe because it is known to help remove mold and mildew)

Mix and store in a dark container — just put a spray top on a half-full hydrogen peroxide bottle. Spray liberally on mold/mildew, let sit for 1–2 hours, rinse and repeat if necessary. If this mixture is ineffective or if you just want to jump to the hard stuff, you can spray hydrogen peroxide straight on mold and mildew as well.

Garbage disposal cleaner
If you have a garbage disposal or kitchen drain, you know it can get a little stinky from time to time. Next time you smell a little something, try this!

- 1/4 cup baking soda
- 1/4 cup lemon juice (fresh or in a jar)

Mix the baking soda and lemon juice together to make a pasty liquid. The liquid will start fizzing — quickly pour down the disposal. Let it sit for at least 5 minutes. Run cold water, turn on the disposal, and run for up to a minute.

Foaming hand soap

- 1–2 cups water (depending on soap container size)
- 1–2 tablespoons castile soap (depending on soap container size)
- 10–20 drops essential oils (depending on soap container size)

Mix and pour ingredients into the soap container and shake to combine — some settling in between uses is to be expected. Pump on hands, lather, and rinse.

Floor Cleaners

So many floors, so little time! There are so many conflicting opinions to the clean floor camp, and if you are washing floors weekly you can definitely do some damage if you don't do it right. I'm going to share a handful of methods and cleaners and you can choose which one works best for you and your particular floor cleaning situation.

Hardwood Floors

Regardless of the type of hardwood floor you have, you need to make sure that you aren't saturating the floors when you wash them. Too much water can ruin surfaces, warp the floors, and get underneath to the subfloor, causing irreparable damage. So don't get them too wet, and if you do get a little too much water on them, keep a towel or microfiber cloth handy to absorb any excess liquid.

What's the big concern with vinegar and hardwood floors? Vinegar is an acid, and hardwood floors need a pH that's neutral or close to it so there isn't any damage. With frequent vacuuming, and not wearing shoes in the house, hardwood floors don't need as much cleaning as other floors need. You can easily get by with a barely damp microfiber pad over the floors weekly and a cleaner as needed. If you have pets, kids, and/or wear shoes in the house, you're going to need to use a little washing solution of some sort weekly or at least biweekly.

What do I clean my own floors with? I mix it up and alternate between a vinegar/water solution and a water/plant-based soap solution. Try them out, see what you prefer or are comfortable with and go from there. Put a little muscle into it, and even the dirtiest of floors will shine with these cleaners. When mixed with water, the solution's acidity is drastically lowered and it becomes an effective method to wash hardwood floors. The vinegar and water mixture cuts through dirt and grime, leaving a streak-free and naturally clean floor.

NOTE: Cleaning floors with vinegar is merely my suggestion, please form your own opinion and try at your own risk. If you are unsure, test in an inconspicuous spot. These recipes are only for *sealed* hardwood floors or prefabricated hardwood floors, not waxed or unfinished hardwoods.

If you have unfinished, waxed, or bamboo hardwood floors, the best approach is to use a barely damp (with water) microfiber mop pad. Always check your manufacturer's instructions first.

Bucket and mop method — vinegar

This is the old-fashioned method to wash floors and works great if you are wanting to get up close and personal with your floors. I don't do this every week, but when I feel like the floors need a really good cleaning, this works great. You can use the mixture on most baseboards, too.

- 1/2 cup white vinegar

- 1 gallon of warm water
- 2–3 drops essential oils

Refillable spray mop or spray bottle — vinegar

Refillable spray mops are super-convenient and work well for daily touch-ups and regular floor cleaning. Make sure that your microfiber pad is rinsed frequently to prevent streaking.

- 3 teaspoons white vinegar
- 16 ounces of warm water
- 1–2 drops essential oils

Other Floors

All-purpose floor cleaner (hardwood floors included) bucket and mop — no vinegar

- 2–3 teaspoons castile or plant-based dish soap
- 1 gallon of warm water
- 2–3 drops essential oils

Add the water to a bucket and then add the soap. Dip your cloth or mop in the bucket, thoroughly wring out tool, and mop. Rinse mop head or cloth frequently and work in sections, drying thoroughly as you go.

Refillable spray mop or spray bottle (hardwood floors included) — no vinegar

- 1–2 drops castile or plant-based dish soap
- 16 ounces warm water
- 1–2 drops essential oils

Add the water to the mop and then add the soap. Spray, mop, and rinse mop head as you go. Work in sections, drying thoroughly as you go.

Laminate floor cleaner

Mix equal parts of:

- white vinegar
- rubbing alcohol
- water

Pour into a spray bottle or refillable spray mop. Spray and wipe floors. This dries quickly because of the alcohol and it cleans and disinfects.

Natural grout cleaner (for floors with tiles and grout)

- 2 teaspoons cream of tartar
- lemon juice or water

Combine the cream of tartar with the lemon juice to make a paste the consistency of runny toothpaste. Apply to the grout and scrub with a stiff bristled cleaning brush. Rinse and wipe dry.

Heavy-duty floor cleaner

This can be used in basements, garages, and on tile and linoleum. Use it when you need a little cleaning boost — you'll love the results.

- 1/4 cup borax
- 1 gallon hot water
- 10 drops essential oils

Mix the borax (make sure you don't inhale the borax powder and keep it away from children), water, and essential oils in a mop bucket, stirring to dissolve. Mop as you normally do. Rinsing is usually not required.

QUICK TIP: A couple helpful tips for streaks and residue on floors: If you are using a microfiber pad, dampen it before starting and rinse often while washing the floors. If you have streaks with a steam mop and rinsing the mop head frequently doesn't solve the problem, you might need to use distilled water (purchase by the gallon at your local grocery or drugstore).

Laundry Cleaners

Laundry soap

Clean clothes with a recipe you can make yourself? Hooray! This recipe yields up to 96 loads of clean laundry.

- 1 bar finely grated castile soap (use a scented one if you'd like)
- 2 cups borax
- 2 cups Arm & Hammer Super Washing Soda
- 1 cup baking soda
- 30 drops essential oils

Combine ingredients in a large container and take care to keep the dust to a minimum.

Carefully pour into a gallon container. Use 1 tablespoon/load for HE (high-efficiency) and 2 tablespoons/load for regular machines. Use 1 tablespoon oxygen bleach powder per load to whiten and brighten as desired.

Fabric Softeners

Most conventional fabric softeners and dryer sheets are not only toxic, but they also coat and build up in the fibers, making clothes and towels harder to clean. If you love your fabric softener and dryer sheets and love that scent that's associated with clean laundry, you probably don't want to make the switch to something natural if it's unscented. I'm right there with you — I want my laundry to smell clean and fresh. Here are four natural ways to scent and soften your laundry:

1. Vinegar (softens)

Add 1/4 cup of white vinegar to the fabric softener dispenser or a fabric softener ball. I love this for sheets and towels — it will make your towels unexpectedly soft and fluffy. If you need a little scent, feel free to add 20–30 drops of your favorite essential oil(s) to about 16 ounces of vinegar. Shake before each use because the oils will separate from the vinegar and you don't want any oil on your laundry.

2. Wool dryer balls (reduce static and lightly scent if you add essential oils)

Wool is naturally antibacterial, making it awesome for using with laundry. Place 3–4 wool dryer balls with each load. Put a couple drops of essential oil on each ball if you'd like a little scent. Most wool dryer balls will last 300–400 uses, so this is a great, inexpensive dryer sheet alternative.

3. Laundry scent boosters (add scent and soften)

If you love those commercial scent boosters this is the recipe for you!

- 1–2 cups Epsom salts (depending on how much you want to make)
- 20–30 drops essential oil
- mason jar

Add 1 tablespoon of the laundry scent booster directly to the washer and wash as usual.

4. DIY flannel mini dryer sheets (add scent to the dryer)

If you *need* to use a dryer sheet, this is a great alternative.

- 20 or so small pieces of flannel or cotton

- 20–30 drops essential oil
- mason jar

Put the flannel or cotton pieces in a container and add essential oils. Keep the lid off until the sheets have completely dried — at least a day or two. Add a sheet or two to each dryer cycle. Wash and refill when the scent has dissipated.

CHAPTER ELEVEN: RESOURCES AND FAVORITES

One of my favorite parts of being a cleaning expert is trying just about every cleaning product on the market. I put a variety of brands side by side and compare them in my home under a variety of conditions and degrees of dirty. Once I've narrowed down different products for a variety of uses, I use them in my home for a while. If I get to the bottom of the cleaner or at the end of the lifespan of a product and I order more, it makes it to my favorites list. Besides the re-order criteria it also has to pass some vigorous testing in my own home:

- Must be safe and natural and rated high on the EWG.org website

- No complaints about the scent of the cleaner — cannot stink
- Cannot break by the use of children
- Has to look good and make me want to clean
- Bonus points if it's made in the USA

If you visit my website, you'll notice that I have my own product line — Clean Mama Home. It's full of my favorites and must-have cleaning products and tools to get you started with natural cleaning. Go to www.cleanmama.net/cleaning-favs and www.cleanmama.net/start-here for the latest!

I know that not everyone will want to clean just like me, so I also share my favorite tools and products along with my favorite resources with my readers. Want to know what makes the cut and what my favorite products and resources are? I share those, too!

If you haven't figured it out by now, next to cleaning and homekeeping, I love list making and getting things done. Lists help me stay focused and keep me from wasting time trying to decide what to clean next. I have three resources on my website that have helped millions of readers just like you stay focused and get things done.

Clean Mama Home: making cleaning

cute and fun! In my shop you'll som
my favorite cleaning supplies — mi
fiber cleaning cloths, bar mop cloths,
glass spray bottles and recipe labels,
notepads, soy-based candles, planners,
binders, and more.

Homekeeping Society: a monthly essentials subscription to help streamline and organize your life. This is my virtual hand-holding, cleaning-right-along-with-you service.

Clean Mama Printables: downloadable lists and organizers designed to help you get things figured out quickly. You'll find a cleaning planner, homekeeping binder kit, shopping lists, menu planning kit, budget and bill paying kit, and other productivity based resources.

Some of My Favorite Products and Brands

Vacuum cleaners: Miele (HEPA filter and bag vacuum) and Dyson cordless

Floor cleaners: Full Circle, Bona, Bissell, Method, Better Life

Carpet cleaners: Bissell, Biokleen

Cleaning tools: Full Circle, Scotch-Brite, OXO, Fuller Brush, Casabella, Grove Collaborative

Dishwasher and laundry tablets: Grab Green, Seventh Generation, Biokleen

Furniture spray, window wash, all-purpose cleaner: Better Life, Murchison-Hume, Caldrea

Detergent, all-purpose bleach alternative, scented vinegar: The Laundress, Four Monks, Aunt Fannie's

Soaps: Dr. Bronner's castile (liquid and bar) and Sal Suds

Essential Oils: doTERRA, Plant Therapy, NOW

Find downloads and additional resources at http://www.cleanmama.net/new-simply -clean.

Enjoying Your Effortlessly Clean and Beautiful Home!

Cleaning can be fun, and a cleaning routine with simple principles and techniques is the best way to take the guesswork out of what needs to be cleaned and when you should clean it. Homekeeping is a lost art — treat it as such and you'll find some unexpected happiness as you clean and organize your home. Go easy on yourself. I hope you've found that even the least cleaning-inclined person can figure out methods for maintaining a clean home and find blissful success. Go back and reread what you need to, mark up this book, and print out checklists to guide you. You're on your way to a cleaning routine that takes care of itself, makes sense, and is full of grace and has plenty of room for life to take center stage. When you need a little reset (everyone does!) use the Quick Home Reset Checklist (page 325) to get you back on track in a hurry.

That's the secret of the Simply Clean method — your life is the focus and a clean and managed home is just a by-product that doesn't get in the way of the things that really matter. Now that you don't have to think about cleaning, you can focus on enjoying your beautifully clean and serene home every day.

Happy cleaning!

QUICK HOME RESET CHECKLIST

Need a quick reset to get you back on track? Use this checklist, add 15–30 minutes a day for a little homekeeping, and in five days you'll be back on track.

Day 1:
Monday

Monday — Bathroom cleaning day

Task: declutter toiletries — go through bathroom cabinets, cupboards, drawers, and counters and toss anything that you no longer use or need.

❏ Make beds	❏ Declutter
❏ Check floors	❏ Do laundry
❏ Wipe counters	

Day 2:
Tuesday

Tuesday — Dusting day

Task: declutter kitchen counters — remove everything from kitchen counters, wash counters thoroughly, and put back only the items that you use and need.

❏ Make beds	❏ Declutter
❏ Check floors	❏ Do laundry
❏ Wipe counters	

Day 3: Wednesday
Wednesday — Vacuuming day
Task: declutter clothes — go through your clothes or those of other family members and gather items that can be donated, passed on, or sold.

❑ Make beds ❑ Check floors ❑ Wipe counters	❑ Declutter ❑ Do laundry

Day 4: Thursday
Thursday — Floor washing day
Task: declutter under the kitchen sink — remove everything, spray and wipe clean, and toss any items that need to go. Return the necessities.

❑ Make beds ❑ Check floors ❑ Wipe counters	❑ Declutter ❑ Do laundry

Day 5: Friday
Friday — Catch-all day
Task: clear surfaces — look for places that clutter collects (bookcases, coffee tables, the kitchen table) and clear and clean the surfaces

❏ Make beds
❏ Check floors
❏ Wipe counters

❏ Declutter
❏ Do laundry

APPENDIX

Daily Cleaning Tasks Checklist
Weekly Cleaning Tasks Checklist
The Simply Clean Method — Daily, Weekly, and Rotating Tasks Reference Checklist
The 7-Day Simply Clean Kick Start Checklist
The 28-Day Simply Clean Challenge Checklist
The 28-Day Simply Clean Challenge + Daily and Weekly Tasks Checklist
Monthly/Rotating Cleaning Tasks Checklist
Spring Cleaning Checklist
Monthly Focus Areas Checklist
Kitchen Speed Cleaning Checklist
Bathroom Speed Cleaning Checklist
Stain Removal Chart
House for Sale Checklist
Quick Home Reset Checklist
Whole-House Declutter Checklist
Unfinished Tasks Checklist
Keep or Toss Checklist

DAILY CLEANING TASKS CHECKLIST

	✓		✓
Make beds		Make beds	
Check floors		Check floors	
Wipe counters		Wipe counters	
Declutter		Declutter	
Do laundry		Do laundry	
Make beds		Make beds	
Check floors		Check floors	
Wipe counters		Wipe counters	
Declutter		Declutter	
Do laundry		Do laundry	
Make beds		Make beds	
Check floors		Check floors	
Wipe counters		Wipe counters	
Declutter		Declutter	
Do laundry		Do laundry	
Make beds		Make beds	
Check floors		Check floors	
Wipe counters		Wipe counters	
Declutter		Declutter	
Do laundry		Do laundry	
Make beds		Make beds	
Check floors		Check floors	
Wipe counters		Wipe counters	
Declutter		Declutter	
Do laundry		Do laundry	

WEEKLY CLEANING TASKS CHECKLIST

	✓		✓
Monday — Bathroom cleaning day		Monday — Bathroom cleaning day	
Tuesday — Dusting day		Tuesday— Dusting day	
Wednesday — Vacuuming day		Wednesday — Vacuuming day	
Thursday — Floor washing day		Thursday — Floor washing day	
Friday — Catch-all day		Friday — Catch-all day	
Saturday — Sheets + towels day		Saturday — Sheets + towels day	
Sunday — Daily cleaning tasks		Sunday — Daily cleaning tasks	

WEEKLY CLEANING TASKS CHECKLIST

	✓		✓
Monday — Bathroom cleaning day		Monday — Bathroom cleaning day	
Tuesday — Dusting day		Tuesday — Dusting day	
Wednesday — Vacuuming day		Wednesday — Vacuuming day	
Thursday — Floor washing day		Thursday — Floor washing day	
Friday — Catch-all day		Friday — Catch-all day	
Saturday — Sheets + towels day		Saturday — Sheets + towels day	
Sunday — Daily cleaning tasks		Sunday — Daily cleaning tasks	

WEEKLY CLEANING TASKS CHECKLIST			
	✓		✓
Monday — Bathroom cleaning day		Monday — Bathroom cleaning day	
Tuesday — Dusting day		Tuesday — Dusting day	
Wednesday — Vacuuming day		Wednesday — Vacuuming day	
Thursday — Floor washing day		Thursday — Floor washing day	
Friday — Catch-all day		Friday — Catch-all day	
Saturday — Sheets + towels day		Saturday — Sheets + towels day	
Sunday — Daily cleaning tasks		Sunday — Daily cleaning tasks	

WEEKLY CLEANING TASKS CHECKLIST			
	✓		✓
Monday — Bathroom cleaning day		Monday — Bathroom cleaning day	
Tuesday — Dusting day		Tuesday — Dusting day	
Wednesday — Vacuuming day		Wednesday — Vacuuming day	
Thursday — Floor washing day		Thursday — Floor washing day	
Friday — Catch-all day		Friday — Catch-all day	
Saturday — Sheets + towels day		Saturday — Sheets + towels day	
Sunday — Daily cleaning tasks		Sunday — Daily cleaning tasks	

THE SIMPLY CLEAN METHOD — DAILY, WEEKLY, AND ROTATING TASKS REFERENCE CHECKLIST

Daily

Completed daily, these tasks are the secret to keeping your home tidy most of the time

- ❏ **Make beds** — make your bed and teach the others in your home to make their beds, too
- ❏ **Check floors** — sweep/vacuum as needed with a broom, vacuum, or microfiber floor duster
- ❏ **Wipe counters** — wipe kitchen counters down after meals and check bathroom counters
- ❏ **Declutter** — pick up clutter during the day and in the evening
- ❏ **Do laundry** — complete one load of laundry from start to finish every day

Weekly
The weekly tasks rotate through the week. Complete as quickly as possible, aiming for 10 minutes. Complete anything lingering on Friday or the next week.
❑ **Monday** — Bathroom cleaning day ❑ **Tuesday** — Dusting day ❑ **Wednesday** — Vacuuming day ❑ **Thursday** — Floor washing day ❑ **Friday** — Catch-all day ❑ **Saturday** — Sheets + towels day ❑ **Sunday** — Daily cleaning tasks

Monthly/Rotating
The monthly/rotating tasks are completed on a monthly, bimonthly, and quarterly basis. Follow the Monthly/Rotating Cleaning Tasks Checklist — for what tasks to complete and when to complete them.
❑ **Vacuum baseboards** — use your nozzle or brush attachment ❑ **Wash baseboards** — wipe thoroughly ❑ **Clean light fixtures** — tackle one room/ area a month ❑ **Wash rugs** — wash bathroom and area rugs

- ❑ **Clean oven** — use self-clean feature on oven or wipe out
- ❑ **Clean refrigerator + freezer** — remove food and wipe thoroughly
- ❑ **Clean appliances** — clean your household appliances (dishwasher, washer + dryer, etc.)
- ❑ **Polish wood furniture** — give your furniture a little extra clean and polish
- ❑ **Spot-clean walls** — wipe away any marks and handprints
- ❑ **Spot-clean furniture** — treat any spots and stains
- ❑ **Rotate/vacuum mattresses** — give your mattresses a little turn and clean
- ❑ **Launder bedding** — wash quilts, duvet covers, pillows
- ❑ **Clean window treatments** — vacuum, wipe, and/or launder any window treatments
- ❑ **Wash windows** — clean inside and out
- ❑ **Replace filters** — furnace, humidifier, dehumidifier, air cleaner, etc.
- ❑ **Wipe switches/phone/remotes** — give those most-touched areas a quick clean

THE 7-DAY SIMPLY CLEAN KICK START CHECKLIST

	✓
Day 1: Decluttering	
Day 2: Bathrooms	
Day 3: Dusting	
Day 4: Vacuuming	
Day 5: Floor washing	
Day 6: Catch-all day	
Day 7: Laundry	

THE 28-DAY SIMPLY CLEAN CHALLENGE CHECKLIST	
	✓
WEEK 1: KITCHEN	
Day 1: Clear and clean kitchen counters	
Day 2: Clean small appliances	
Day 3: Purge and clean refrigerator and freezer	
Day 4: Clean oven and wipe appliance fronts	
Day 5: Clear and clean pantry or food storage area	
Day 6: Empty, declutter, and clean at least two drawers and cupboards (or one of each)	
Day 7: Catch-all day	

THE 28-DAY SIMPLY CLEAN CHALLENGE CHECKLIST

WEEK 2: LIVING SPACES	
Day 8: Clear all flat surfaces	
Day 9: Dust light fixtures	
Day 10: Dust corners, vents, and baseboards	
Day 11: Deep vacuum — vacuum edges and under furniture	
Day 12: Declutter and clean storage areas	
Day 13: Launder throws, pillows, and blankets	
Day 14: Catch-all day	
WEEK 3: BATHROOMS	
Day 15: Declutter all surfaces	
Day 16: Dust light fixtures	
Day 17: Vacuum floors, baseboards, and vents	
Day 18: Wash floors and baseboards	
Day 19: Empty, declutter, and clean at least two drawers or cupboards (or one of each)	

THE 28-DAY SIMPLY CLEAN CHALLENGE CHECKLIST	
Day 20: Take inventory of bathroom linens — donate, toss, or keep	
Day 21: Catch-all day	
WEEK 4: BEDROOMS	
Day 22: Declutter and dust all surfaces	
Day 23: Thorough vacuuming	
Day 24: Vacuum and wash baseboards	
Day 25: Clean and vacuum under beds	
Day 26: Purge any unused/unwanted clothing	
Day 27: Wash pillows and bedding	
Day 28: Catch-all day	

THE 28-DAY SIMPLY CLEAN CHALLENGE + DAILY AND WEEKLY TASKS CHECKLIST

WEEK 1: KITCHEN

Day 1: Clear and clean kitchen counters	Day 2: Clean small appliances
Sunday — Daily cleaning tasks	Monday — Bathroom cleaning day
❏ Make beds ❏ Check floors ❏ Wipe counters ❏ Declutter ❏ Do laundry	❏ Make beds ❏ Check floors ❏ Wipe counters ❏ Declutter ❏ Do laundry
Day 3: Purge and clean refrigerator and freezer	Day 4: Clean oven and wipe appliance fronts
Tuesday — Dusting day	Wednesday — Vacuuming day
❏ Make beds ❏ Check floors ❏ Wipe counters ❏ Declutter ❏ Do laundry	❏ Make beds ❏ Check floors ❏ Wipe counters ❏ Declutter ❏ Do laundry

Day 5: Clear and clean pantry or food storage area	Day 6: Empty, declutter, and clean at least two drawers and cupboards (or one of each)
Thursday — Floor washing day	Friday — Catch-all day
❏ Make beds ❏ Check floors ❏ Wipe counters ❏ Declutter ❏ Do laundry	❏ Make beds ❏ Check floors ❏ Wipe counters ❏ Declutter ❏ Do laundry

Day 7: Catch-all day
Saturday — Sheets + towels day
❏ Make beds ❏ Check floors ❏ Wipe counters ❏ Declutter ❏ Do laundry

WEEK 2: LIVING SPACES	
Day 8: **Clear all flat surfaces**	**Day 9:** **Dust light fixtures**
Sunday — Daily cleaning tasks	Monday — Bathroom cleaning day
❏ Make beds ❏ Check floors ❏ Wipe counters ❏ Declutter ❏ Do laundry	❏ Make beds ❏ Check floors ❏ Wipe counters ❏ Declutter ❏ Do laundry
Day 10: **Dust corners, vents, and baseboards**	**Day 11:** **Deep vacuum — edges and under furniture**
Tuesday — Dusting day	Wednesday — Vacuuming day
❏ Make beds ❏ Check floors ❏ Wipe counters ❏ Declutter ❏ Do laundry	❏ Make beds ❏ Check floors ❏ Wipe counters ❏ Declutter ❏ Do laundry

Day 12: Declutter and clean storage areas	Day 13: Launder throws, pillows, and blankets
Thursday — Floor washing day	Friday — Catch-all day
❏ Make beds ❏ Check floors ❏ Wipe counters ❏ Declutter ❏ Do laundry	❏ Make beds ❏ Check floors ❏ Wipe counters ❏ Declutter ❏ Do laundry

Day 14: Catch-all day
Saturday — Sheets + towels day
❏ Make beds ❏ Check floors ❏ Wipe counters ❏ Declutter ❏ Do laundry

WEEK 3: BATHROOMS	
Day 15: Declutter all surfaces	**Day 16: Dust light fixtures**
Sunday — Daily cleaning tasks	Monday — Bathroom cleaning day
❏ Make beds ❏ Check floors ❏ Wipe counters ❏ Declutter ❏ Do laundry	❏ Make beds ❏ Check floors ❏ Wipe counters ❏ Declutter ❏ Do laundry
Day 17: Vacuum floors, baseboards, and vents	**Day 18: Wash floors and baseboards**
Tuesday — Dusting day	Wednesday — Vacuuming day
❏ Make beds ❏ Check floors ❏ Wipe counters ❏ Declutter ❏ Do laundry	❏ Make beds ❏ Check floors ❏ Wipe counters ❏ Declutter ❏ Do laundry

Day 19: Empty, declutter, and clean at least two drawers or cupboards (or one of each)	Day 20: Take inventory of bathroom linens: donate, toss, or keep
Thursday — Floor washing day	Friday — Catch-all day
❏ Make beds ❏ Check floors ❏ Wipe counters ❏ Declutter ❏ Do laundry	❏ Make beds ❏ Check floors ❏ Wipe counters ❏ Declutter ❏ Do laundry

Day 21: Catch-all day
Saturday — Sheets + towels day
❏ Make beds ❏ Check floors ❏ Wipe counters ❏ Declutter ❏ Do laundry

WEEK 4: BEDROOMS	
Day 22: **Declutter and dust** **all surfaces**	**Day 23:** **Thorough** **vacuuming**
Sunday — Daily cleaning tasks	Monday — Bathroom cleaning day
❏ Make beds ❏ Check floors ❏ Wipe counters ❏ Declutter ❏ Do laundry	❏ Make beds ❏ Check floors ❏ Wipe counters ❏ Declutter ❏ Do laundry
Day 24: **Vacuum and wash** **baseboards**	**Day 25:** **Clean and vacuum** **under beds**
Tuesday — Dusting day	Wednesday — Vacuuming day
❏ Make beds ❏ Check floors ❏ Wipe counters ❏ Declutter ❏ Do laundry	❏ Make beds ❏ Check floors ❏ Wipe counters ❏ Declutter ❏ Do laundry

Day 26: Purge any unused/ unwanted clothing	Day 27: Wash pillows and bedding
Thursday — Floor washing day	Friday — Catch-all day
❏ Make beds ❏ Check floors ❏ Wipe counters ❏ Declutter ❏ Do laundry	❏ Make beds ❏ Check floors ❏ Wipe counters ❏ Declutter ❏ Do laundry

Day 28: Catch-all day
Saturday — Sheets + towels day
❏ Make beds ❏ Check floors ❏ Wipe counters ❏ Declutter ❏ Do laundry

MONTHLY/ROTATING CLEANING TASKS CHECKLIST

Complete these monthly rotating cleaning tasks when it works for you and your schedule. The most efficient way to complete these tasks is to pair them with weekly cleaning tasks when you are able. If you're vacuuming on Wednesday, vacuum the baseboards at the same time. If you're washing floors on Thursday, wash your throw rugs as you're gathering them to wash the floors.

JANUARY

- ❏ Vacuum baseboards
- ❏ Vacuum + spot-clean furniture
- ❏ Clean light fixtures — kitchen
- ❏ Wash rugs
- ❏ Polish wood furniture
- ❏ Change filters
- ❏ Clean oven
- ❏ Wash windows — inside + out
- ❏ Wipe down appliances

FEBRUARY

- ❏ Vacuum baseboards
- ❏ Wash baseboards
- ❏ Vacuum + spot-clean furniture
- ❏ Clean light fixtures — living/dining rooms

- ❏ Wash rugs
- ❏ Polish wood furniture
- ❏ Wipe switches/phones/remotes
- ❏ Spot-clean walls
- ❏ Wipe down appliances

MARCH

- ❏ Vacuum baseboards
- ❏ Vacuum + spot-clean furniture
- ❏ Clean light fixtures — family room
- ❏ Wash rugs
- ❏ Polish wood furniture
- ❏ Dust ceilings and corners
- ❏ Wash/fluff pillows + bedding
- ❏ Turn/rotate/vacuum mattresses
- ❏ Wipe down appliances

APRIL

- ❏ Vacuum baseboards
- ❏ Vacuum + spot-clean furniture
- ❏ Clean light fixtures — bathrooms
- ❏ Wash rugs
- ❏ Polish wood furniture
- ❏ Clean oven
- ❏ Wipe switches/phones/remotes
- ❏ Launder draperies
- ❏ Wipe down appliances

MAY

- ❑ Vacuum baseboards
- ❑ Wash baseboards
- ❑ Vacuum + spot-clean furniture
- ❑ Clean light fixtures — main bedroom
- ❑ Wash rugs
- ❑ Polish wood furniture
- ❑ Clean window treatments
- ❑ Spot-clean walls
- ❑ Wipe down appliances

JUNE

- ❑ Vacuum baseboards
- ❑ Vacuum + spot-clean furniture
- ❑ Clean light fixtures — other bedrooms
- ❑ Wash rugs
- ❑ Polish wood furniture
- ❑ Change filters
- ❑ Clean oven
- ❑ Wash windows — inside + out
- ❑ Wipe down appliances

JULY

- ❑ Vacuum baseboards
- ❑ Vacuum + spot-clean furniture
- ❑ Clean light fixtures — kitchen
- ❑ Wash rugs
- ❑ Polish wood furniture
- ❑ Clean oven
- ❑ Dust ceilings and corners

- ❏ Clean refrigerator + freezer
- ❏ Wipe down appliances

AUGUST

- ❏ Vacuum baseboards
- ❏ Wash baseboards
- ❏ Vacuum + spot-clean furniture
- ❏ Clean light fixtures — living/dining rooms
- ❏ Wash rugs
- ❏ Polish wood furniture
- ❏ Wipe switches/phones/remotes
- ❏ Spot-clean walls
- ❏ Wipe down appliances

SEPTEMBER

- ❏ Vacuum baseboards
- ❏ Vacuum + spot-clean furniture
- ❏ Clean light fixtures — family room
- ❏ Wash rugs
- ❏ Polish wood furniture
- ❏ Clean window treatments
- ❏ Wash/fluff pillows + bedding
- ❏ Turn/rotate/vacuum mattresses
- ❏ Wipe down appliances

OCTOBER

- ❏ Vacuum baseboards
- ❏ Vacuum + spot-clean furniture
- ❏ Clean light fixtures — bathrooms
- ❏ Wash rugs

- ❏ Polish wood furniture
- ❏ Wipe switches/phones/remotes
- ❏ Vacuum garage
- ❏ Vacuum basement/storage area
- ❏ Wipe down appliances

NOVEMBER

- ❏ Vacuum baseboards
- ❏ Wash baseboards
- ❏ Vacuum + spot-clean furniture
- ❏ Clean light fixtures — main bedroom
- ❏ Wash rugs
- ❏ Polish wood furniture
- ❏ Dust ceilings and corners
- ❏ Spot-clean walls
- ❏ Wipe down appliances

DECEMBER

- ❏ Vacuum baseboards
- ❏ Vacuum + spot-clean furniture
- ❏ Clean light fixtures — other bedrooms
- ❏ Wash rugs
- ❏ Polish wood furniture
- ❏ Wipe switches/phones/remotes
- ❏ Spot-clean walls
- ❏ Wipe down appliances

SPRING CLEANING CHECKLIST

Use this thorough checklist to spring clean your entire home in 31 tasks or days. Use it how it works for you and your schedule and you'll be opening the windows and letting in that fresh air in no time.

Get ready	✓
Declutter your cleaning supply storage	
Clean under bathroom and kitchen sinks	
Gather your tools — make a spring cleaning caddy	
Whole house	✓
Dust corners, edges, and ceilings with a long-handled duster	
Clean doors and doorknobs	
Clean light switches and switch plates	
Vacuum and wipe baseboards	
Wash hard surface floors	
Vacuum/clean floor and wall vents	
Dust ceiling fans and light fixtures	
Clean window blinds and window treatments	
Wash windows and clean window casings	

Deep clean/shampoo carpets	
Living areas	✓
Clean lamps and lampshades	
Launder pillows and throws and/or fluff them in the dryer	
Thoroughly dust all surfaces	
Vacuum under furniture	
Kitchen	✓
Empty and clean at least one cupboard and drawer	
Wash/wipe cupboard doors and drawers	
Clean refrigerator and freezer	
Clean oven, microwave, and dishwasher	
Clean small appliances	
Clean pantry/food storage area	
Scrub sink and faucet	
Bedrooms	✓
Clean lamps and lampshades	
Thoroughly dust all surfaces	
Clean and vacuum under beds	
Fluff and/or launder pillows, bedding, and blankets	

Bathrooms	✓
Thoroughly clean toilets, sinks, tubs, and showers	
Wash cupboard and drawer fronts	
Wash bath mats, rugs, window treatments, and shower curtains	

January:
Whole-House Declutter

Follow the **Whole-House Declutter Checklist** on page 377 for a more detailed list.

❑ **Declutter** — do a quick whole-house declutter and gather at least 3 bags you can get rid of

❑ **Clean surfaces** — remove clutter from flat surfaces (counters, dressers, etc.)

❑ **Sort** — sort through any existing paper piles that are out on counters or surfaces

❑ **Mail** — deal with your mail situation and come up with a way to sort through mail daily so it doesn't pile up

❑ **Kitchen** — declutter counters, cabinets, and drawers

❑ **Bathroom(s)** — declutter counters, toiletries, cabinets, and drawers

❑ **Bedroom(s)** — declutter surfaces, linens, and clothing

❑ **Living areas** — declutter toys, storage, and flat surfaces

❑ **Other areas** — declutter attic, basement, garage, and/or storage areas

February:
Kitchen

- ❏ **Declutter** — completely clear counters and wipe clean
- ❏ **Clean surfaces** — wipe cabinet and drawer fronts
- ❏ **Deep clean** — clean refrigerator, freezer, and oven
- ❏ **Food storage** — clean pantry or food storage area — discard any expired food
- ❏ **Toss or donate** — items that are no longer needed or wanted
- ❏ **Organize** — group like items together
- ❏ **Contain** — use pretty containers to make food and cooking supplies more attractive
- ❏ **Label** — to make locating items easier and to unify the space
- ❏ **Scrub** — scrub the kitchen sink
- ❏ **Clean most-touched areas** — wipe knobs, doors, and handles

March:
Spring Cleaning

Follow the **Spring Cleaning Checklist** on page 154 for a more detailed list.
- ❏ **Declutter** — clear surfaces and lose anything you don't use or love

- ❏ **Clean surfaces** — dust and/or clean all surfaces
- ❏ **Light fixtures and lamps** — dust and/or clean all light fixtures, lamps, and shades
- ❏ **Window treatments** — dust and/or launder window treatments and blinds
- ❏ **Clean + fluff** — rotate/flip mattresses and clean pillows, blankets, and bedding
- ❏ **Clean floors** — thoroughly vacuum and wash all floors
- ❏ **Clean most-touched areas** — wipe handles, light switches/switch plates, knobs, doors, remotes, and phones
- ❏ **Deep clean** — carpeted areas, wash windows, wash doors, and wash baseboards

April: Bathrooms

- ❏ **Declutter** — clear bathroom surfaces of any unnecessary items
- ❏ **Clean** — clean and wipe all surfaces (counters, toilets, showers, bathtubs)
- ❏ **Deep clean** — vacuum and wash baseboards and floors
- ❏ **Dust** — dust and clean light fixtures
- ❏ **Window treatments** — dust and/or launder window treatments and blinds
- ❏ **Clean** — shower curtains and bath mats

- ❏ **Clean most-touched areas** — wipe handles, knobs, doors, and switches/switch plates
- ❏ **Stock up** — plan ahead and stock up on toilet paper, tissues, and toiletries
- ❏ **Practice** — take it out, put it away with toiletries and any items on the counters
- ❏ **Ambience** — add something special — new towels, a candle, container for cotton balls, etc.

May:
Garage or basement

- ❏ **Declutter** — clear surfaces and lose anything you don't use or love
- ❏ **Clean** — dust and/or clean all surfaces
- ❏ **Sweep or vacuum** — clean garage floor
- ❏ **Organize** — put systems in place that will get your household through the summer
- ❏ **Wash vehicles** — wash or take to be washed
- ❏ **Vacuum floors** — thoroughly vacuum and clean vehicle floors
- ❏ **Clean most-touched areas** — wipe handles, knobs, doors, and switches/switch plates
- ❏ **Deep clean** — wash vehicle windows, clean dashboard, empty trunk, etc.

June:
Bedroom(s)

- ❏ **Declutter** — clear surfaces and lose anything you don't use or love
- ❏ **Clean surfaces** — dust and/or clean all surfaces
- ❏ **Evaluate** — what is/isn't working — write it down and plan it out
- ❏ **Light fixtures and lamps** — dust and clean all light fixtures, lamps, and shades
- ❏ **Clean + fluff** — pillows, blankets, and bedding
- ❏ **Fresh start** — thoroughly vacuum and/or wash floors
- ❏ **Relax** — add items to encourage calm and relaxation. Make sure the bedside table(s) are cleaned off and add a book that's been on your list to read.

July:
Organizing Systems

- ❏ **Declutter** — clear surfaces and lose anything you don't use or love
- ❏ **Evaluate** — look at methods and systems already in place
- ❏ **Find 3 trouble spots** — write them down and commit to taking care of them

- ❏ **Something new** — choose a new method or way of doing something to simplify your life
- ❏ **Perspective** — ask a friend for ideas or take pictures to see it in a new light
- ❏ **Supplies** — shop the house for supplies to put your new systems in place
- ❏ **Set up your systems** — show family members how to implement
- ❏ **Add on** — once the first system is in place and working, add the next one

August:
Closets

- ❏ **Declutter** — completely empty and clean the space
- ❏ **Clean surfaces** — clean and wipe shelves and wash/vacuum the floor
- ❏ **Evaluate** — what is/isn't working — write it down and plan it out
- ❏ **Toss or donate** — items that are no longer needed, wanted, or don't fit
- ❏ **Organize** — group like items together
- ❏ **Label** — to make locating items easier and more uniform
- ❏ **Practice** — take it out, put it away to keep it neat and tidy going forward

September:
Entryway or Mudroom

- ❏ **Declutter** — completely empty and clean the entryway (coat closet, bench, etc.)
- ❏ **Clean** — clean and wipe shelves and wash/vacuum the floor and outside entry area
- ❏ **Evaluate** — what is/isn't working — add storage and make sure you have a place to hang guests' coats
- ❏ **Organize + contain** — group like items together
- ❏ **Practice** — take it out, put it away
- ❏ **Slipper basket** — if you want to make your guests feel especially comfortable and keep shoes at the door, add a basket with socks or slippers for them to slip on upon arrival
- ❏ **Garment care kit** — keep a lint roller, sweater shaver, and any garment care items in a basket for any clothing mishaps

October:
Laundry Room or Area

- ❏ **Declutter** — clear laundry room or laundry area of unnecessary items
- ❏ **Clean** — clean and wipe any shelves or drawers
- ❏ **Deep clean** — washer and dryer

- ❑ **Evaluate** — what is/isn't working
- ❑ **Toss or donate** — items that are no longer needed or wanted
- ❑ **Organize** — group like items together
- ❑ **Contain** — use pretty containers to make supplies more attractive
- ❑ **Label** — to make locating items easier and to unify the space
- ❑ **Practice** — take it out, put it away, and do a load of laundry every day to keep it manageable

November:
Living Areas

- ❑ **Declutter** — clear surfaces and lose anything you don't use or love
- ❑ **Clean surfaces** — dust and/or clean all surfaces
- ❑ **Light fixtures and lamps** — dust and clean all light fixtures, lamps, and shades
- ❑ **Window treatments** — dust and/or launder window treatments and blinds
- ❑ **Clean + fluff** — pillows, blankets, and cushions
- ❑ **Fresh start** — thoroughly vacuum and wash floors if necessary
- ❑ **Clean most-touched areas** — wipe handles, knobs, doors, remotes, and phones

❑ **Ambience** — add items to encourage family time and relaxation — games, books, pillows, a candle, etc.

December:
Office/Paperwork

Follow the **Keep or Toss Checklist** on page 381 for a more detailed list.

❑ **Declutter** — clear surfaces and lose anything you don't use or love

❑ **Evaluate** — look at methods and systems already in place

❑ **Find 3 trouble spots** — write them down and commit to taking care of them

❑ **Something new** — choose a new method to simplify your paper situation

❑ **Shred, shred, shred** — follow the **Keep or Toss Checklist** on page 381 for guidelines

❑ **Supplies** — shop the house for supplies to put your new systems in place

❑ **Set up your systems** — whether it's a new filing system or an attempt to go paperless, get something in place that will cut down on paper

KITCHEN SPEED CLEANING CHECKLIST

Use this checklist for after-dinner cleanup or just as a reference for how to get this job done in a hurry.

Set a timer — Eliminate any distractions and set a timer for 10–15 minutes.	
Quick declutter — Collect anything on the counters and kitchen table that doesn't belong. Don't worry about putting these items away right now.	
Unload/load dishwasher — If you have dishes on the counter or sink, load them in the empty dishwasher.	
Clean the sink — Give your sink a little scrub. You'll be amazed how this simple task can impact your kitchen cleanliness.	
Wipe surfaces — Spray counters and the kitchen table and wipe clean with a cloth or sponge. Once you're in the habit of wiping down counters daily, this is a simple and manageable task.	
Check the stove for any spills — If you see any spills or burned-on food, quickly wipe them away.	

Quick sweep or vacuum — Check under the table and in the corners for any crumbs that can be quickly swept up.	
Put out fresh hand and dish towels — The final touch to the clean kitchen is a fresh towel.	

BATHROOM SPEED CLEANING CHECKLIST	
Use this checklist for your weekly bathroom cleaning routine or for when you need to get this job done quickly.	
Counters and sinks — Clear off your counters and sinks	
Mirrors — Spray and wipe clean. I recommend a glass and mirror microfiber cloth for lint- and streak-free mirrors. Keep this cloth handy and reuse in each bathroom.	
Sink, toilet, and bathtub or shower — Quickly spray with your disinfecting cleaner. If you don't use a tub or shower regularly, you don't need to clean it weekly.	
Toilet — Do a quick clean with your preferred toilet cleaner and brush.	
Repeat these steps in each bathroom. Once you've done that, go back to the first bathroom and complete these steps:	

Sink, toilet, and bathtub or shower — Wipe off the cleaner using a separate cloth or paper towel for each to avoid cross contamination. Don't forget to clean the base of your toilets too!	
Place dirty cloths in a container and discard the paper towels.	
Repeat these steps in each bathroom.	

STAIN REMOVAL CHART

With a quick response, most stains can be removed. Here are some of my favorite ways to remove common stains. Once you've tried the method, launder as usual.

Bodily fluids — Blot and soak up with cold water and treat with oxygen bleach alternative.

Fruit and juice — Run under warm water and treat the stain with white vinegar. If the fabric is white, treat with hydrogen peroxide.

Grease and oil — Keep a piece of white chalkboard chalk in the laundry room and draw over any grease stains. If the grease or oil stain is larger, sprinkle a little cornstarch over the stain and a drop of dish soap.

Ink — Dab with a cotton swab dipped in rubbing alcohol.

Sweat — Mix up a baking soda and water paste and scrub with a clean toothbrush to dissolve perspiration. Soak in 1/4 cup oxygen bleach alternative and warm water in washing machine or a small laundry bucket for a couple hours or overnight.

Unknown stains — Rub with a bar of castile soap.

Wine — Blot with club soda or cool water and soak up stain.

HOUSE FOR SALE CHECKLIST

GET YOUR HOUSE READY
TO SELL

- ❑ Declutter house
- ❑ Pack up unnecessary belongings
- ❑ Clean walls
- ❑ Clean light fixtures
- ❑ Check light fixtures
- ❑ Wash windows
- ❑ Wash baseboards
- ❑ Clean window treatments
- ❑ Clean mirrors
- ❑ Wipe switch plates
- ❑ Clean appliances — inside + out
- ❑ Deep clean kitchen
- ❑ Clean off counters (kitchen/bath)
- ❑ Deep clean bathrooms
- ❑ Remove personal items (pictures)
- ❑ Remove cobwebs — basement, garage, porch
- ❑ Check/fix caulk in bathrooms
- ❑ Clean carpets and floors
- ❑ _____
- ❑ _____
- ❑ _____
- ❑ _____
- ❑ _____
- ❑ _____

QUICK CLEAN CHECKLIST
FOR SHOWINGS

- ❑ Wipe down kitchen counters
- ❑ Wipe fronts of appliances
- ❑ Quick vacuum floors where needed
- ❑ Quick wash floors where needed
- ❑ Wipe down bathroom counters
- ❑ Clean toilets
- ❑ Put out clean towels
- ❑ Fluff pillows on sofas
- ❑ Make beds — arrange pillows
- ❑ Open window treatments
- ❑ Quick dust
- ❑ Burn a candle or use air freshener
- ❑ Take out all garbage
- ❑ Put out clean rugs
- ❑ Open window for fresh air
- ❑ Pick up toys and personal items
- ❑ Hide dirty laundry — take it with you if you need to!
- ❑ _____
- ❑ _____
- ❑ _____
- ❑ _____
- ❑ _____
- ❑ _____
- ❑ _____
- ❑ _____

QUICK HOME RESET CHECKLIST

Need a quick reset to get you back on track? Use this checklist, add 15–30 minutes a day for a little homekeeping, and in five days you'll be back on track.

Day 1:
Monday

Monday — Bathroom cleaning day

Task: declutter toiletries — go through bathroom cabinets, cupboards, drawers, and counters and toss anything that you no longer use or need.

❏ Make beds ❏ Check floors ❏ Wipe counters	❏ Declutter ❏ Do laundry

Day 2:
Tuesday

Tuesday — Dusting day

Task: declutter kitchen counters — remove everything from kitchen counters, wash counters thoroughly, and put back only the items that you use and need.

❏ Make beds ❏ Check floors ❏ Wipe counters	❏ Declutter ❏ Do laundry

Day 3: Wednesday
Wednesday — Vacuuming day
Task: declutter clothes — go through your clothes or those of other family members and gather items that can be donated, passed on, or sold.

❑ Make beds	❑ Declutter
❑ Check floors	❑ Do laundry
❑ Wipe counters	

Day 4: Thursday
Thursday — Floor washing day
Task: declutter under the kitchen sink — remove everything, spray and wipe clean, and toss any items that need to go. Return the necessities.

❑ Make beds	❑ Declutter
❑ Check floors	❑ Do laundry
❑ Wipe counters	

Day 5: Friday
Friday — Catch-all day
Task: clear surfaces — look for places that clutter collects (bookcases, coffee tables, the kitchen table) and clear and clean the surfaces

❏ Make beds	❏ Declutter
❏ Check floors	❏ Do laundry
❏ Wipe counters	

WHOLE-HOUSE DECLUTTER CHECKLIST

Need a little direction in your decluttering? Use this checklist as a guide to declutter your whole house. Complete one task a day or a handful of tasks when you have time. Work at your own pace and enjoy a decluttered home.

	✓		✓
Do a quick whole-house declutter — try to fill three garbage bags to the brim with clutter		Shoes	
		Luggage	
		Purses and bags	
		Toys	
Remove clutter from surfaces		Entryway	
Sort existing paper piles		Coats and outerwear	
File paperwork — create a system		Garage	
Refrigerator		Attic, basement, storage areas	
Freezer			
Food storage containers			

Kitchen counters			
Kitchen cupboards			
Kitchen drawers			
Pantry or food storage			
Kitchen small appliances			
Under the kitchen sink			
Laundry area			
Bathroom counters			
Bath and shower products			
Bathroom toiletries			
Bathroom cupboards			
Bathroom drawers			
Bathroom towels			
Linens and bedding			
Clothing			

UNFINISHED TASKS CHECKLIST

Use this checklist to jot down any tasks you want to complete as you're working your way through *Simply Clean.* Don't let a little task slow you down — write it down and come back to it.

Task to be completed	Date completed
Task to be completed	Date completed
Task to be completed	Date completed
Task to be completed	Date completed
Task to be completed	Date completed

Task to be completed	Date completed
Task to be completed	Date completed
Task to be completed	Date completed
Task to be completed	Date completed
Task to be completed	Date completed

KEEP OR TOSS CHECKLIST

When sorting through papers and files, it's hard to know what to keep and what to toss — this little checklist should help! This is a general list. Different circumstances may apply to your specific paper pile.

1 MONTH	❏ Receipts for nondeductible items ❏ Deposit and ATM withdrawal slips ❏ Reconciled bank statements — most of this information is online; keep the paper copy if you want a written record at home
1–3 YEARS	❏ Checkbook ledgers for business expenses/ payments ❏ Cancelled checks — if your bank returns them ❏ Mortgage statements ❏ Insurance records ❏ Charitable contributions and donation receipts ❏ All business- and income-related documents ❏ Proof or receipts of all tax-deductible purchases

7+ YEARS	❏ State and federal income tax returns ❏ W-2s and 1099s ❏ Medical bills and statements — especially showing proof of payment ❏ Any receipts that were used as tax deductions in the case of an audit ❏ Cancelled checks or bank statements saved digitally ❏ Mileage records, if you take the deduction ❏ Real estate tax forms and records ❏ Tax supporting documents — the IRS recommends keeping these for at least 6 years after filing if an error is suspected

FOREVER	❏ Birth certificates ❏ Marriage/divorce papers ❏ Auto titles ❏ Mortgage statements ❏ Investment statements ❏ Passports ❏ Receipts from major purchases for home improvement (for insurance claim information in the case of a loss) ❏ Wills ❏ Current life insurance policies ❏ Medical records ❏ Education records ❏ Pension and retirement plans ❏ Contracts ❏ Property agreements

ACKNOWLEDGMENTS

What an unexpected twist — from elementary art teacher to cleaning and homekeeping expert. This book is my love for teaching and homekeeping all wrapped up in one neat and tidy little package. I know that God's hand has been in the entire process and for that I am eternally grateful.

Thank you, thank you . . .

There are not enough words to express my love for my husband, George, and our three children. Thank you for your support in this little dream (that I didn't dare to dream) of mine.

To my sister, assistant, and best friend, Abby, for adding perspective and laughter, simplifying my life, and for just being awesome.

To my parents — thank you for believing in me and always supporting my business ventures from making my own sticker books in fifth grade to selling sheets of ice door-to-door from a sled. You definitely honed my entrepreneurial spirit.

To my family and friends — thank you for your support, prayers, and encouragement. What a blessing you have been!

To Maria Ribas, my amazing agent — you have been such a dream to work with and I know that this book is here because of all the work you put in to it.

To Reni and the whole Bliss and Tell Branding Company — Clean Mama wouldn't be what it is without you!

To the publishing team at Touchstone — what a surreal and seamless experience. Your vision and insight for this book have been spot-on. What a delight you have been to work with!

To my blog community and readers — without you, Clean Mama would be just me and a toilet brush. Thank you for showing up and cleaning right alongside me. Your excitement for cleaning a little bit every day is contagious!

To you, the reader — thank you for purchasing this book. I hope that it blesses you and your home. May it be a handbook for your home — worn, marked-up, loved, and a true sign of some happy cleaning!

ABOUT THE AUTHOR

Betty Rapinchuk is a cleaning expert, a wife and mom to three, a successful entrepreneur, and a former art teacher. She's the blogger behind *Clean Mama,* the leading online homekeeping community, and advises the world's leading lifestyle brands — Martha Stewart, *Real Simple, Better Homes & Gardens,* SC Johnson, Bissell, and Scotch-Brite — on how to clean up life's little and big messes. She's also the go-to girl for the over twenty million readers who follow her online and buy her books, paper goods, and signature cleaning products.

The employees of Thorndike Press hope you have enjoyed this Large Print book. All our Thorndike, Wheeler, and Kennebec Large Print titles are designed for easy reading, and all our books are made to last. Other Thorndike Press Large Print books are available at your library, through selected bookstores, or directly from us.

For information about titles, please call:

(800) 223-1244

or visit our Web site at:

http://gale.cengage.com/thorndike

To share your comments, please write:
Publisher
Thorndike Press
10 Water St., Suite 310
Waterville, ME 04901